OPPOSING
VIEWPOINTS®
SERIES

Mental Illness

Other Books of Related Interest:

Opposing Viewpoints Series

Juvenile Crime

Terminal Illness

Addiction

Current Controversies Series

The Elderly

Medical Ethics

At Issue Series

Anorexia

Antidepressants

Are Americans Overmedicated?

Attention Deficit Hyperactivity Disorder

Prescription Drugs

Treating the Mentally Ill

What Causes Addiction?

"Congress shall make no law ... abridging the freedom of speech, or of the press."

First Amendment to the U.S. Constitution

The basic foundation of our democracy is the First Amendment guarantee of freedom of expression. The Opposing Viewpoints Series is dedicated to the concept of this basic freedom and the idea that it is more important to practice it than to enshrine it.

OPPOSING VIEWPOINTS® SERIES

Mental Illness

Mary E. Williams, Book Editor

GREENHAVEN PRESS

An imprint of Thomson Gale, a part of The Thomson Corporation

Detroit • New York • San Francisco • New Haven, Conn. • Waterville, Maine • London

MAR 1 5 2007

THOMSON
——————✳——————™
GALE

Christine Nasso, *Publisher*
Elizabeth Des Chenes, *Managing Editor*

For more information, contact:
Greenhaven Press
27500 Drake Rd.
Farmington Hills, MI 48331-3535
Or you can visit our Internet site at http://www.gale.com

LIBRARY OF CONGRESS CATALOGING-IN-PUBLICATION DATA

Mental Illness / Mary E. Williams, book editor.
   p. cm. -- (Opposing viewpoints)
  Includes bibliographical references and index.
  ISBN-13: 978-0-7377-2947-4 (lib. : alk. paper)
  ISBN-10: 0-7377-2947-3 (lib. : alk. paper)
  ISBN-13: 978-0-7377-2948-1 (pbk. : alk. paper)
  ISBN-10: 0-7377-2948-1 (pbk. : alk. paper)
  1. Mental illness. 2. Mental illness--United States. 3. Psychology, Pathological. I. Williams, Mary E., 1960-
  RC454.M39 2007
  362.2--dc22

              2006020106

Printed in the United States of America
10 9 8 7 6 5 4 3 2 1

Contents

Chapter 3: What Mental Health Issues Do Youths Face?

Chapter 4: What Treatments for Mental Illness Are Effective?

Why Consider Opposing Viewpoints?

"The only way in which a human being can make some approach to knowing the whole of a subject is by hearing what can be said about it by persons of every variety of opinion and studying all modes in which it can be looked at by every character of mind. No wise man ever acquired his wisdom in any mode but this."

John Stuart Mill

In our media-intensive culture it is not difficult to find differing opinions. Thousands of newspapers and magazines and dozens of radio and television talk shows resound with differing points of view. The difficulty lies in deciding which opinion to agree with and which "experts" seem the most credible. The more inundated we become with differing opinions and claims, the more essential it is to hone critical reading and thinking skills to evaluate these ideas. Opposing Viewpoints books address this problem directly by presenting stimulating debates that can be used to enhance and teach these skills. The varied opinions contained in each book examine many different aspects of a single issue. While examining these conveniently edited opposing views, readers can develop critical thinking skills such as the ability to compare and contrast authors' credibility, facts, argumentation styles, use of persuasive techniques, and other stylistic tools. In short, the Opposing Viewpoints Series is an ideal way to attain the higher-level thinking and reading skills so essential in a culture of diverse and contradictory opinions.

In addition to providing a tool for critical thinking, Opposing Viewpoints books challenge readers to question their own strongly held opinions and assumptions. Most people form their opinions on the basis of upbringing, peer pressure, and personal, cultural, or professional bias. By reading carefully balanced opposing views, readers must directly confront new ideas as well as the opinions of those with whom they disagree. This is not to simplistically argue that everyone who reads opposing views will—or should—change his or her opinion. Instead, the series enhances readers' understanding of their own views by encouraging confrontation with opposing ideas. Careful examination of others' views can lead to the readers' understanding of the logical inconsistencies in their own opinions, perspective on why they hold an opinion, and the consideration of the possibility that their opinion requires further evaluation.

Evaluating Other Opinions

To ensure that this type of examination occurs, Opposing Viewpoints books present all types of opinions. Prominent spokespeople on different sides of each issue as well as well-known professionals from many disciplines challenge the reader. An additional goal of the series is to provide a forum for other, less known, or even unpopular viewpoints. The opinion of an ordinary person who has had to make the decision to cut off life support from a terminally ill relative, for example, may be just as valuable and provide just as much insight as a medical ethicist's professional opinion. The editors have two additional purposes in including these less known views. One, the editors encourage readers to respect others' opinions—even when not enhanced by professional credibility. It is only by reading or listening to and objectively evaluating others' ideas that one can determine whether they are worthy of consideration. Two, the inclusion of such viewpoints encourages the important critical thinking skill of objectively evaluating an author's credentials and bias. This evaluation will illuminate an author's reasons for taking a particular stance on an issue and will aid in readers' evaluation of the author's ideas.

It is our hope that these books will give readers a deeper understanding of the issues debated and an appreciation of the complexity of even seemingly simple issues when good and honest people disagree. This awareness is particularly important in a democratic society such as ours in which people enter into public debate to determine the common good. Those with whom one disagrees should not be regarded as enemies but rather as people whose views deserve careful examination and may shed light on one's own.

Thomas Jefferson once said that "difference of opinion leads to inquiry, and inquiry to truth." Jefferson, a broadly educated man, argued that "if a nation expects to be ignorant and free . . . it expects what never was and never will be." As individuals and as a nation, it is imperative that we consider the opinions of others and examine them with skill and discernment. The Opposing Viewpoints Series is intended to help readers achieve this goal.

David L. Bender and Bruno Leone,
Founders

Introduction

> *"The 'psycho' label's poisonous stigma remains far too potent."*
>
> —Robert David Jaffee

> *"Getting rid of the stigma of all behaviors labeled 'mental illness' would be a surefire way to ensure their increase in perpetuation."*
>
> —Richard E. Vatz

According to an often-cited survey funded by the National Institute of Mental Health (NIMH), about 25 percent of Americans develop a mental illness in any given year, and nearly 50 percent experience mental health problems at some time in their lives. The most common illnesses include anxiety disorders such as social phobia and panic disorder (experienced by 29 percent of survey participants at some time in their lives), impulse-control disorders such as attention-deficit hyperactivity disorder (experienced by 25 percent of participants), and depression (experienced by 21 percent of those surveyed). The NIMH contends that a majority of these cases are mild, requiring little or no therapy. The conductors of the survey also found, however, that each year, about one out of every seventeen people develops a severe mental disorder that requires immediate treatment. According to Harvard University epidemiologist Ronald C. Kessler, most of these people do not seek professional help—or they receive poor-quality care when they do seek treatment.

In seeking to discover why the mentally ill face such challenges in finding the assistance they need, some analysts point to the stigma that remains attached to mental illness. Many people perceive mental illness as a form of personal weakness, as a devastating disgrace, or as potentially dangerous. As Les Campbell, a volunteer with the Alliance for the Mentally Ill, points out, "Out of our fear of the unknown, the mentally ill are reduced in our minds from potentially valuable citizens to tainted eccentrics at best and fearsome maniacs at worst. [In] years past, they were chained, straitjacketed and hidden away in hospitals. When one escapes, it is too often reported, 'Somewhere, homeless on the streets . . . is a dangerous psychotic.'" Even though the great majority of mentally ill people are not physically violent, media fixations on psychotic criminals and "escaped lunatics" influence the American public's view of mental illness. Not wanting to be viewed as weak, strange, or dangerous, the mentally ill often avoid seeking the assistance that might label them as social outcasts.

Campbell believes that improved education would help to destigmatize mental illness in the United States. If health-education classes in high schools were to include accurate information about mental illness, people might feel less threatened if they themselves or a loved one developed a serious mental disorder. The attitudes toward the mentally ill in other nations, such as Belgium, suggest that a more informed approach is possible. "In Geel, Belgium, the mentally ill live with 900 foster families where they work and take part in the community," notes Campbell. According to Franz Vaneynde, the secretary of the foster family program in Geel, "The sole difference that distinguishes this community from others is that the culturally conditioned, deep-seated fear of the mentally ill does not exist here."

Many psychiatrists believe that the best way to destigmatize the mentally ill is to view mental diseases as primarily biological disorders caused by a combination of genetic, neurochemical, and social factors. "Our brains are biological organs by their very nature," says Paul Appelbaum, former president of the American Psychiatric Association. "Any disorder is in its essence a biological process." This understanding of mental illness deflects the notion that mental disorders are basically character flaws or in some way the ill person's "fault." In addition, providing the mentally ill with greater access to effective psychotherapy and improved psychiatric drugs would reduce the most distressing symptoms of mental disorders, Appelbaum and others assert. Tackling the symptoms of mental illness through medication and learning life skills and coping strategies through therapy enhances a patient's confidence and social skills, they maintain.

Some critics, however, question whether the destigmatization of mental illness is a worthy goal. Richard E. Vatz, associate editor of *USA Today* magazine, published by the Society for the Advancement of Education, believes that stigma plays an important role in preventing phony or frivolous claims of mental illness. He contends that "stigmatization as a negative reinforcer can have a salutary effect, minimizing needless visits to mental health professionals." Those who truly need mental health care—such as schizophrenics—have symptoms so severe that they are not deterred from seeking treatment, he maintains.

These concerns over the stigmatization and treatment of the mentally ill are connected to the even larger question of how mental illness should be defined. Psychiatrists, psychologists, therapists, and patients continue to debate whether mental illnesses are primarily medical diseases with medical solutions or disorders springing from various social, cultural, and environmental factors. This question and many others are examined in the following chapters: How Serious a Problem Is Mental Illness? How Should Society Address Mental Illness? What Mental Health Issues Do Youths Face? What Treatments for Mental Illness Are Effective? In these chapters a variety of commentators and experts offer perspective on the social, legal, and medical issues facing the mentally ill.

CHAPTER 1

How Serious a Problem Is Mental Illness?

Chapter Preface

According to a widely cited 2004 national mental health study, the prevalence of mental illness in the United States is disturbingly high. This particular study—the National Comorbidity Survey Replication (NCS-R)—collects results through a household census taken every ten years by researchers at Harvard University, the University of Michigan Institute for Social Research, and the National Institute of Mental Health (NIMH). According to survey director Ronald C. Kessler, 55 percent of Americans will experience a mental disorder at some point in their lives, and many of these illnesses will go untreated. Furthermore, despite an increase in mental health awareness among the public and the advent of improved medications, people who eventually seek treatment for mental illness often receive substandard care, Kessler contends.

Interviewers asked participants—a broad cross-section of 9282 Americans over the age of eighteen—whether they had experienced episodes of extended sadness, alcohol or drug abuse, irrational fears, or disturbing or unusual behavioral symptoms. If so, investigators inquired further about these experiences, noting how long the symptoms lasted and how they had impacted the participants' lives. Researchers concluded that the most common mental illnesses were mood disorders such as depression and bipolar disorder, affecting 21 percent of people at some point in their lives, and substance abuse, affecting 15 percent. Social anxiety disorder, classified as a phobia, troubles 12 percent. In addition, one quarter of those surveyed had experienced a mental illness during the previous year. "The key point to remember is that mental disorders are highly prevalent and chronic," says Thomas Insel, chief of the NIMH. Noting that the onset of mental illness typically occurs between adolescence and age thirty, Insel says that the study "demonstrates clearly that these really are the chronic disorders of young people in this country."

Some psychiatrists argue, however, that these statistics are inflated and that mental illness is too broadly defined. In response to the national mental health survey, Johns Hopkins psychiatrist Paul McHugh says, "Fifty percent of Americans are mentally impaired—are you kidding me?" The real problem, McHugh contends, is that "the diagnostic manual we are using in psychiatry is like a field guide and it just keeps expanding and expanding." Indeed, critics claim, the *Diagnostic and Statistical Manual of Mental Disorders*, 4th edition (DSM-IV)—used by doctors, therapists, and health insurers as a reference of mental illnesses—includes behaviors exhibited by nearly everyone. Skeptics point out that the DSM-IV lists problems such as insomnia, worrying, restlessness, getting drunk, arrogance, seeking approval, poor grammar, feeling sad, and holding grudges as possible signs of mental illness. While critics recognize that it is the combination and severity of such symptoms that determine whether a person is mentally ill, the organization of the DSM-IV increases the chances that personality flaws will be defined as mental disorders. As McHugh quips, "Pretty soon, we'll have a syndrome for short, fat Irish guys with a Boston accent, and I'll be mentally ill."

It is difficult to determine the pervasiveness of mental illness because mental health experts do not agree on its definition. While some believe that mental impairments occur as frequently as physical illnesses, others maintain that mental disorders requiring a doctor's attention are fairly rare. The authors in the following chapter continue this debate on the prevalence of mental illness, questioning the accuracy of survey techniques, stressors that might contribute to mental disorders, and whether the mentally ill receive adequate care.

> "The United States likely ranks first in the world in the rate of mental illnesses."

Mental Illness Is Prevalent in America

Paul D. Lawrence

Mental illness is prevalent in the United States, maintains Paul D. Lawrence in the following viewpoint. The capitalist system is a significant cause of mental illness because it creates economic insecurity and despair—although biological, environmental, and cultural stresses are also contributing factors, he notes. Lawrence contends that a socialist political system would more effectively promote mental health. If the profit motive were removed from the research and treatment of mental disorders, the mentally ill would receive better care, he concludes. Lawrence writes for The People, *a newspaper published by the Socialist Labor Party.*

As you read, consider the following questions:

1. According to Lawrence, what are some of the barriers to treating mental illness in America?
2. How might "nature and nurture" interact to create mental illness, according to the author?

Paul D. Lawrence, "U.S. Leads the World—In Mental Illness," *The People*, November–December 2005, p. 8. Reproduced by permission.

3. Why have biological explanations for mental illness become popular in the United States, in Lawrence's opinion?

The United States likely ranks first in the world in the rate of mental illnesses, according to a yet incomplete study. Within the past year [2005], 25 percent of Americans met the criteria for having a mental illness. One-quarter of them had an illness so severe that it disrupted daily functioning.

The problem is far worse than that. The survey excluded schizophrenics, who likely suffer the most severe mental illness. Many are hospitalized; others are homeless and walk around talking aloud to themselves.

Less than half who need treatment get it, and what that half gets is generally inadequate. Barriers to treatment include inadequate health care or insurance and the still lingering stigma of "mental illness."

Many Do Not Get Help

Effective treatments for many disorders exist. However, many sufferers fail to seek professional help. "You wouldn't rely on your priest for treatment if you had breast cancer," said Thomas Insel, chief of the National Institute of Mental Health, which is funding the study. "Why would you go to your priest for a major depressive disorder? These are real medical and brain disorders, and they need to be treated that way."

In a way, these statistics are not surprising. The United States is the world's foremost capitalist nation. Capitalism is an insane system. Therefore, there should be many mental illnesses. The increase in mental illness in China as that nation moves to capitalism suggests that this logic is not far-fetched.

Nature and Nurture

An explanation is, however, not quite so simple. It requires some consideration of the dynamics of mental illness. Insel's reference to "brain disorders" is likely not 100 percent correct. Nature and nurture both play roles.

The staff of the Mayo Clinic notes that depression, for example, may spring from purely biological factors. It may also come from stresses in life, such as the death of a loved one or, we might add, loss of a job or an overbearing boss.

"We don't yet know if the underlying neurochemical aspects of these two depressive reactions are the same," the Mayo clinic staff continues. "In other words, one person may have a mental illness because of their nature—their genetic vulnerabilities, their neurochemical functioning. And another person may have a mental illness because of nurture—an environmental cause that perhaps then alters their neurochemistry. Most of the time, however, it's probably a complex interaction of both nature and nurture."

Another case would be alcoholism. Alcoholics have a biological inability to metabolize alcohol as efficiently as the nonalcoholic does. That eventually leads to uncontrolled drinking unless the disorder is successfully treated. Yet, a person unable to metabolize alcohol growing up in a society that discourages or forbids alcohol, such as Saudi Arabia or, in the United States, Utah, would not likely develop alcoholism.

Cultural factors may be extremely significant. The *Washington Post* reported:

"Patients with schizophrenia, a disease characterized by hallucinations and disorganized thinking, recover sooner and function better in poor countries with strong extended family ties than in the United States, two long-running studies by the World Health Organization have shown."

In the *Communist Manifesto*, [Karl] Marx and [Friedrich] Engels noted "the practical absence of the family among proletarians." As in many cases, they foresaw tendencies that would grow to maturity with the ripening of capitalism. Single parenthood, divorce, relocation of family members to other

Percentage of Americans Who Will Have Specific Disorders in Their Lifetimes

DISORDER	LIFETIME PREVALENCE
Any anxiety disorder	**28.8%**
Panic disorder	4.7%
Agoraphobia without panic	1.4%
Specific phobia	12.5%
Social phobia	12.1%
Generalized anxiety disorder	5.7%
Post-traumatic stress disorder	6.8%
Obsessive-compulsive	1.6%
Separation anxiety	5.2%
Mood disorder	**20.8%**
Major depression	16.6%
Dysthymia	2.5%
Bipolar I or II	3.9%
Impulse-control disorder	**24.8%**
Oppositional-defiant disorder	8.5%
Conduct disorder	9.5%
Attention deficit hyperactivity	8.1%
Intermittent explosive	5.2%
Substance disorder	**14.6%**
Alcohol abuse	13.2%
Alcohol dependence	5.4%
Drug abuse	7.9%
Drug dependence	3.0%

Ronald C. Kessler, Harvard University, 2004.

parts of the country, often due to economic necessity, have left little of the traditional family that might give support.

The Medical Model

The biological model *has* made advances in the treatment of mental illness, in particular the development of medications that can alter the way the brain functions and better, if not cure, the condition. The medical model is quite popular with the pharmaceutical industry, as TV ads for Prozac demonstrate.

That model is also popular with health care insurers. "Insurance companies found that paying for pills was cheaper and simpler than paying therapists to address the interpersonal causes of suffering—especially because general physicians could write most of the prescriptions," the *Washington Post* reported.

The *Post* also noted factors that are more benign in the acceptance of the medical model. "Patient advocates realized that defining mental illnesses as brain diseases reduced the stigma attached to depression and psychoses—a patient could hardly be blamed for having an organic disease."

Biological factors are important, as the successful treatment of many disorders by medications proves. To focus on them exclusively, however, is incorrect, as the Mayo Clinic noted. Moreover, it lets capitalism off the hook.

The Insanity of Capitalism

Economic insecurity—unemployment or the threat of it, wages inadequate to meet expenses that force some workers to hold two or even three jobs, unrelenting pressure to work faster and produce more—cause many working-class people to become mentally ill, perhaps aided by biological propensities. The news itself provides enough to push others over the brink. Wars and the threats of war for the sake of capitalist interests, environmental pollution and global warming are not happy thoughts, nor is the impossibility of doing much about them as long as capitalism lasts. To workers who are not class conscious these problems seem retractable, even insurmountable. Low turnout for elections indicates despair with the capitalist parties, if not with capitalism itself.

The sanity of socialism can replace the insanity of capitalism, with salutary effects for the useful producers. Instead of being driven harder to produce more wealth for the exploiters and receive a relatively—and perhaps now even absolutely—diminishing share of that wealth, the useful producers will receive the full social value of their labor.

Ample provision will be made for rearing children and supporting the elderly and those unable to engage in production. Economic security will be supplemented by the elimination of the other baneful effects of capitalism, such as mentioned above.

Where biological factors alone cause mental illness, humane care will replace the inhumanity of capitalism. Homeless schizophrenics will not be in the asylums of the streets. Research, unfettered by the profit motive, will produce better drugs and perhaps even determine the source of the biological causes of illness before symptoms emerge. In disorders like alcoholism, those susceptible to the disorder could receive education and counseling to discourage them from beginning to drink. If this sounds too good to be true, it isn't. All that is necessary is for workers to organize their power politically and economically to replace capitalism and establish socialism. The mental illnesses caused or aggravated by capitalism will disappear with the madness of capitalism itself.

| *"Diagnostic exaggeration dogs psychiatry today."*

The Prevalence of Mental Illness in America Has Been Exaggerated

Paul McHugh

In the following viewpoint Paul McHugh disputes a recent Harvard Medical School survey claiming that a majority of Americans suffer mental illness in their lifetime. This study is deeply flawed, he argues, because it was conducted by inexperienced technicians who simply recorded certain symptoms, such as anxiety or depression, without connecting these symptoms to possible causes. As McHugh notes, such symptoms may be a reaction to certain stressful or disappointing life events—not necessarily a sign of mental illness. McHugh is a professor of psychiatry and behavioral science at the Johns Hopkins University School of Medicine.

As you read, consider the following questions:

1. How do internists diagnose illnesses today, according to the author?

2. What is problematic about the official *Diagnostic and Statistical Manual of Mental Disorders*, in McHugh's opinion?

3. What would be a productive way to conduct psychiatric research, in the author's view?

As the *New York Times* reported [in 2005], psychiatric epidemiologists from the Harvard Medical School have published studies purporting to demonstrate that some 55 percent of Americans suffer from mental illness in their lifetime. These studies—which cost $20 million, most of it out of the taxpayer's pocket—are based on a survey of 9,282 randomly selected English-speaking subjects over the age of 18 who were seen in their homes by technicians trained to ask specific questions about symptoms believed to indicate mental illnesses. The results led Thomas Insel, director of the National Institute of Mental Health, the studies' primary sponsor, to note that indeed "mental disorders are highly prevalent and chronic." More than half the people of the United States, in other words, have been or are mentally ill. What should we make of this?

Not to put too fine a point on it, we should take the studies' conclusions with a huge grain—perhaps a silo would be required—of salt. Diagnostic exaggeration dogs psychiatry today and will not subside until research psychiatrists use ways closer to those of practicing clinicians for recognizing mental disorders and differentiating the serious from the trivial in mental life. Let me explain.

A Flawed Survey

The survey technicians were instructed to fill in a questionnaire by asking the subjects about mental symptoms such as depression and anxiety that they might have experienced in their lives. Such technicians, sticking to the prescribed inventory, essentially act as secretaries, recording what people say they recall from their past. The techs gather no sense of the persons they are meeting—no appreciation of their life circumstances, the issues they have dealt with, what strengths they brought to bear, or what vulnerabilities they overcame, in dealing with the good and bad fortune life brought them. The individual's family, social circumstances, temperament, character, opportunities, successes, and disappointments are all outside the attention of these interrogators.

Instead, the technicians run down their checklist of symptoms with no thought to causes, simply recording a yes or no answer to each. This is not a psychiatric examination; it is barely a census. The assessment does not rest on a trusting relationship, it presumes honesty and openness in the replies, and it assumes that both the subjects and the technicians understand the questions the same way the experts who constructed the inventory did. Finally, by focusing solely on symptoms—indications of disease or disorder—these inventories tend to direct attention to human frailty rather than to human strengths and to emphasize the burdens and obscure the gifts that life has brought these subjects.

At Johns Hopkins, we became aware of these problems after the last national attempt to do a census of the mentally ill—the so-called Epidemiological Catchment Area Study (ECA) of the early 1980s. We followed up similar questionnaires with a complete examination by qualified psychiatrists of a sample of the subjects previously assessed. These examinations produced diagnoses that failed miserably to match those generated by the less thorough and clinically inexperienced technicians. The questionnaires depicted individuals who were distressed but could neither accurately identify the nature of their distress nor make confident claims about any mental impairment. Nothing in the present study indicates that its expanded version of the old questionnaires can do any better at diagnosing the subjects.

Spinning the Data

Today, experts have become so adept at phrasing their questions that the "target subjects," as we ordinary people are called, generally are unaware just how much they are divulging. The result is a behavioral baseline—retained in databases for posterity.

All that remains is the spin some entity wishes to inflict on the data collected. That's what behavioral researchers did with [the] NIMH [National Institute of Mental Health] study. Although the researchers' conclusions may be outrageous, their data doubtless contains some kernels of truth. Spin is all about interpretation, how various data points are juxtaposed to reflect whatever substantiates the position of those funding the study.

Beverly K. Eakman, New American, *December 29, 2003.*

Poor Diagnostic Methods

But this simply raises the question, why would anyone dream that an inventory of psychic aches and pains would reliably identify mental impairments and distinguish them from the kinds of mental distresses that are part of every person's life?

In addition to relying solely on respondents' yes or no answers to a checklist, the investigators are committed to employing the official *Diagnostic and Statistical Manual of Mental Disorders—Fourth Edition* (abbreviated DSM-IV), which bases all psychiatric diagnoses on symptoms and their course, not on any fuller knowledge of the person. It is as if public health investigators studying the prevalence of pneumonia over time in the American population were satisfied to call every instance of a cough with a fever and a mucoid sputum a case of pneumonia.

Internal medicine gave up on symptom-based diagnosis more than a hundred years ago, replacing it with diagnosis that rests on knowledge of pathology and what produces it. Thus, internists no longer speak of coughs as racking, brassy, or productive, but as produced by viral or bacterial infection, allergies, or vascular congestion. They no longer differentiate Tertian, Quotidian, and Continuous Fevers but fevers from infection, neoplasia, dehydration, and so on.

DSM-IV makes no attempt to classify mental symptoms or complaints by cause. As a result, it mingles serious and impairing conditions with other forms of mental distress in one hopeless and scientifically indigestible stew. When this diagnostic method is employed for a census of mental disorders in the citizenry, it ominously exaggerates the incidence and the nature of mental troubles. It leaves the public wondering: If more than 50 percent of Americans have at some point been mentally "impaired," what constitutes a "normal" mental life?

A Mental Health Field Guide?

Another way of stating the problem is that DSM-IV is the medical counterpart of a naturalist's field guide—say, Roger Tory Peterson's *Field Guide to the Birds*. To develop his guide, Peterson asked expert bird watchers what features of shape, coloring, voice, and range they used to distinguish one warbler from another, and he arranged his guidebook accordingly. As a result, bird watchers became more precise in the terms they used to describe what they saw. But as Peterson noted, amateurs relying on the way birds look often confuse varieties with separate species, while ornithologists turn to biology to make more fundamental distinctions.

Similarly, clinical psychiatrists in 1980 wanted to find a way to apply their diagnostic terms consistently. With DSM-IV, they agreed on which symptoms they would use as criteria for each diagnosis, and thus increased their diagnostic consistency. But the best clinicians apply DSM-IV diagnostic terms only after they have fully examined the patient and come to see these symptoms in context. They do not simply run down a checklist of symptoms, count them up, and attach a diagnosis, as did the technicians from Harvard.

Psychiatrists are right now rewriting the diagnostic manual. I believe they will move closer to internal medicine, classifying patients according to what has provoked their symptoms rather than according to the symptoms alone. Only then will scientific and epidemiologic studies in psychiatry improve.

A Better Way to Research

In the meantime, while scientists are working to lift psychiatry beyond the level of a field guide, epidemiologists should stop expending time and money repeating surveys that purport to measure the prevalence of psychiatric disorders but instead only mislead and alarm the public. They should spend their efforts in more productive areas of psychiatric research.

They might, for example, start following people over time, as cohorts with particular life circumstances: They might consider the long-term performance of children with particular classroom-identified dispositions or children exposed to various forms of deprivation or trauma early in life, seeking to discover how these people manage the hurdles they face and which vulnerabilities to mental problems and which resiliencies they manifest in later life. Epidemiologists should attend to studies where patients with particular characteristics—such as temperament, upbringing, or stress—are compared with nonpatients with similar characteristics (so called case-control studies) testing whether these characteristics provoke, protect against, or are incidental to the patients' mental unrest or illness. They should enhance cross-cultural knowledge of how mental impairment, as opposed to mental distress, is expressed by people of differing cultures and exactly what measures help to prevent or treat the case examples.

Analytic studies like these could accomplish much more than descriptive surveys that do little in the long run but exasperate the public and make ephemeral headlines. Along the way, with these more specific studies we would likely discover not that the majority of people are impaired but just how remarkably resilient most of us are and what distinct and wonderful assets most people bring to life. To conduct more of the same kind of empty surveys as are now being done is, I'm afraid, a little crazy—with crazy defined as doing the same thing again and again and expecting a different result.

| "*Many patients are denied access to . . . new medications simply because of their high cost.*"

The Mentally Ill Are Often Denied Access to Effective Medicines

Matthew W. Nelson

Mentally ill people are often denied the medicines that would help them the most, writes Matthew W. Nelson in the following viewpoint. Many safer and more effective medicines have been recently created, the author explains, but they may not be approved for use by health maintenance organizations (HMOs) because of their high cost. Ironically, these policies that restrict access to better drugs do not actually cut costs, notes Nelson, because patients who use less expensive and less effective medicine incur more costs in the long run if they experience side effects, prolonged illness, or repeated hospitalizations. Nelson is a researcher and an assistant professor of psychiatry at the University of Maryland's School of Medicine in Baltimore.

As you read, consider the following questions:

1. In what ways have medicines for mental illness improved over the past two decades, according to Nelson?
2. What are "fail first" policies, according to the author?
3. In Nelson's opinion, what factors should be taken into account when choosing a psychiatric medication?

In today's economically conscious healthcare climate, attention is increasingly focused on new means to curb costs. The mental health arena has not escaped this scrutiny. An estimated 18.5% of American adults suffer from a diagnosable mental illness in a given year. While one may argue that the cost of treating individuals with mental disorders is high, the lack of, or inappropriate, treatment carries a much higher monetary burden. Illness-related costs, such as lost productivity, total billions of dollars annually.

Over the past couple of decades, there has been an impressive expansion in the knowledge and understanding of mental illness treatment. Moreover, several new classes of pharmacologic agents (for example, the atypical antipsychotics) for use in the treatment of various mental disorders like schizophrenia have also become available. More than just facsimiles of previous medications, many of these agents have offered improvements in safety, tolerability, and clinical outcomes. Because of these advancements, we are now better equipped to successfully achieve control over the symptoms of these diseases. In addition, many other novel agents are in the development and approval processes and, hopefully, will further expand treatment options in the near future.

Despite the fact that these advancements in pharmacologic treatment are beneficial, they come at a cost. New medications still protected under patent laws carry a much higher price than the older medications that are available generically. These cost differences notwithstanding, many of the newer psychotropic agents are considered first-line treatment for a variety of psychiatric disorders; therefore, the cost is justified by the benefits they offer, such as increased effectiveness or fewer adverse effects. Yet many patients are denied access to some of these new medications simply because of their high cost.

Limited Access to Medicine

There are several ways that a patient's access to psychiatric medications may be limited. One method is the use of restricted formularies or "preferred medication lists." Hospital systems or health maintenance organizations (HMOs) may allow the prescribing of only certain medications from each therapeutic drug class, greatly limiting access. If a clinician wishes to use a nonformulary psychotropic, special forms may need to be completed and submitted to an individual or a committee for prior authorization. But even following proper procedures to request a nonformulary medication does not always guarantee that the request will be approved. The difficulty in navigating the system and the time required to do so is often a sufficient deterrent to physicians and patients wanting to use a restricted medication.

Alternatively, HMOs may allow prescriptions for nonformulary drugs, but will charge patients higher copayments than for drugs on a preferred list. This, too, can successfully dissuade patients from using newer psychotropics, by giving preference to cheaper, older drugs.

"Fail first" policies are another mechanism designed to limit medication access in an attempt to control costs. With this approach, patients must try one or more of the less expensive drugs before they are eligible to receive the desired medication. Some fail-first policies are more subtle. They employ purported "treatment algorithms" that are, in reality, cost-control measures. These costbased "algorithms" suggest a less expensive medication as first-line therapy when a more expensive agent, in fact, might be an equivalent or superior clinical choice. When an organization or institution requires

Difficulties Faced by the Mentally Ill

Sitting in the waiting room is a patient begging for a medical bed because he has been evicted from his apartment for failing to pay rent that uses most of his $600 a month income. He is too ill to survive on the streets and only a doctor's letter can win him [a] cot in the corner of a shelter. . . . One patient must ride multiple buses to get here, often risking being assaulted, another has no phone so I can't tell him his lithium level is toxic; and one can only come to see me every six months because he cannot afford the gas and lodging to travel from his remote rural home and the accommodations program has been cut. . . . One of my patients has been sober for a year and making great progress . . . but he has an outstanding fine for a failure to appear in court over a minor infraction . . . and now faces jail.

Cynthia M. A. Geppert, Psychiatric Times, *March 1, 2005.*

mandatory adherence to these cost algorithms, or when clinicians are pressured to follow them, these supposed therapeutic tools become nothing more than a fail-first policy.

Restrictive Measures Do Not Cut Costs

The question then raised is whether these restricted formularies and other limited-access policies are actually successful in cutting costs. [Researchers S.D.] Horn and colleagues looked at this question across a variety of common physical illnesses and found that the more restrictive an organization's medication formulary, the higher the overall healthcare costs. This was reflected not only in the increased number of office visits and hospitalizations but, surprisingly, the more restrictive formularies were associated with higher prescription costs and an increase in the number of prescriptions filled.

Another large study, comparing two organizations in California with restrictive medication practices to one with open access, reported similar results. The organization that had no limitations on access to medications had lower overall costs, as well as lower prescription costs.

Although medications only comprise a small percentage of the total costs of treating mental disorders, they continue to be a primary focus for reducing costs, often through restricted access. Drug therapy is considered an easy target, because the cost associated with prescriptions is tangible and easily calculated. On the other hand, determining the monetary costs of other healthcare resources, such as emergency room visits or nursing care, is not as straightforward.

A Shortsighted Strategy

Sometimes pharmacists and administrators embrace the idea of restricting medication use for budgetary purposes because pharmacy and medication costs are frequently allocated in a budget separate from other healthcare system costs. Attempting to reduce pharmacy costs by limiting access to psychiatric medications, while simultaneously ignoring the consequences to other areas of mental health spending, is shortsighted and can have an enormous impact on the overall economics of treating patients with mental illnesses. In other words, reductions in the pharmacy budget can significantly increase the mental health budget and vice versa; thus, both budgets cannot be viewed as separate, independent entities. Using a less expensive medication and attempting to save a few dollars today can end up costing thousands of dollars tomorrow for other expenses, such as prolonged or repeated hospitalizations.

From a mental health perspective, some argue that the response to psychotropics is idiosyncratic and that similar percentages of patients respond to any given drug within a medication class. Therefore, they contend, using the least expensive drug first is economically sound. These arguments, however, fail to account for individual differences among patients or among medications. Many factors need to be taken into account when choosing a medication for therapy. The patient's comorbid illnesses, potential drug interactions, the drug's side-effect profile, and its effectiveness in illness subsets all require consideration. Failure to recognize these variables can lead to adverse reactions, treatment noncompliance, poor outcomes, and reduced quality of life. Often under-recognized, but equally important when selecting a psychotropic agent, is the clinician's own experience in treating a disorder. Familiarity with the subtle distinctions presented in the illness and among drugs can be invaluable.

As the struggle to achieve parity for mental-health insurance coverage continues, individuals suffering from a mental illness already face difficulties in receiving appropriate treatment. Placing barriers to any treatment option that may ultimately benefit those patients should be avoided. Pharmacists and administrators need to re-examine their efforts to curtail costs by limiting access and availability to certain psychotropics, which may prove more costly when the larger picture is evaluated. Most importantly, patients rely heavily on the treatment decisions made by their trusted clinicians, and every effort should be taken to advocate for the best available treatment options.

> *"[Western] countries are facing epidemic levels of citizens hooked on tranquilizers as well as antidepressants."*

Medicines for Mental Illness Are Overprescribed

B.K. Eakman

B.K. Eakman is executive director of the National Education Consortium and the author of Cloning of the American Mind. *In the following viewpoint she argues that Europeans and North Americans, particularly women, are too often given prescriptions for tranquilizers and antidepressants. Eakman claims that these drugs are addictive and often have debilitating and dangerous side effects. Physicians' unwillingness to address problems that are not easily diagnosable as well as advertising by drug companies are partly to blame for the overuse of these drugs, writes Eakman. In addition, she maintains that women have become exhausted by the feminist claim that they should "have it all," and are taking too many psychiatric drugs as a result.*

As you read, consider the following questions:

1. According to the *Wall Street Journal*, cited by the author, what percentage of French women take tranquilizers or antidepressants?

B.K. Eakman, "Anything That Ails You," *Chronicles*, August 2004, vol. 28, no. 8, pp. 20–21.

2. In Eakman's opinion, why are insurance companies partly to blame for the overuse of psychiatric drugs?

3. Why are school counselors increasingly referring teenage girls to psychotherapists, according to the author?

As far back as the 1970's, shortly after the feminist movement was launched, it was estimated that as many as 30 million American women were taking tranquilizers. That was almost half of the female population at the time. In 1975 alone, more than 103 million prescriptions for tranquilizers were written.

By the 1980's, prescription levels had spiked again. Women throughout Europe and North America were prescribed about twice as many psychotropic drugs as were men. Many of these drugs were taken long-term. In the case of the "minor tranquilizers" (technically, benzodiazepines such as Librium, Valium, Mogadon, and Ativan), continued use was largely the result of drug dependence.

A May 2001 report by the National Institute on Drug Abuse (NIDA) on prescription-drug abuse and addiction stated that studies indicate that "women were more likely than men to be prescribed an abuse-prone prescription drug, particularly anti-anxiety drugs—in some cases 48 percent more likely."

Addiction to Unnecessary Drugs

Overall, men and women have roughly similar rates of nonmedical use of prescription drugs. Young women, however, have demonstrated an increased susceptibility over time to the use of medically unnecessary psychotherapeutic drugs. Be it a sedative, an anti-anxiety drug, or an hypnotic, women are almost twice as likely to become addicted.

Studies from 2001 have estimated that two percent of Americans, or about four million people, have used benzodiazepines regularly for five or more years, a figure matched in the United Kingdom and in Europe. Research also shows that, for senior citizens, benzodiazepines are more frequently prescribed to women, which is now suspected to be the cause of increased falls and fractures among that age group.

The drugged-female problem is a free-world phenomenon. In Britain alone, 60 percent of all minor tranquilizers prescribed in 1987 were consumed by women, and some 17 million people were legally prescribed benzodiazepines in 1999.

A *Wall Street Journal* article on February 25, 2004, claimed that one in every four French women is taking a tranquilizer or an antidepressant and that the average Belgian takes seven times as many sedatives as Americans [do]. Because of the low costs of drugs and little oversight, Western European countries are facing epidemic levels of citizens hooked on tranquilizers as well as antidepressants. . . .

Who Is to Blame?

The tremendous upsurge in tranquilizing drugs seems to have as much to do with the medical profession's reticence to spend time on patient complaints that are not easily diagnosed as it does on advertising by drug companies to create a market for their wares. Insurance companies, in turn, are at least partially to blame for cutting short the amount of time a doctor spends with his patient.

In the United Kingdom in 2003, half a million people were long-term dependents of benzodiazepines, drugs deemed so addictive that official prescription guidelines were saying they should not be taken for more than 28 days in succession. Data from coroners' reports compiled by Britain's Home Office were showing benzodiazepines as a more frequent contributing factor to cases of unnatural death each year than cocaine, heroin, ecstasy, and all other *illegal* drugs.

"Wonder Drugs"?

Today, antidepressants are replacing tranquilizers as the mood-altering drug of choice, based on the questionable notion that anxious, restless, agitated, irritable, and diagnosis-starved patients are actually suffering from depression. Originally touted as being as "harmless as aspirin," the so-called minor tranquilizers have since been found to be addictive, psychologically and/or physically. Thus the rise of the new "wonder drugs," antidepressants, which supposedly act on serotonin levels in the brain to alter personality and behavior. Compounds that target this chemical are known as selective serotonin reuptake inhibitors (SSRI's).

These "harmless" antidepressants have recently been linked to violent behavior, loss of impulse control, and suicidal thoughts. . . .

Prescriptions of benzodiazepines peaked in 1977 in the United Kingdom at 30 million, yet, in 2002, there were still 12.5 million prescriptions. The story in the United States is the same, only the numbers are even greater. Alprazolam, a benzodiazepine originally marketed by Upjohn (now part of Pfizer) as Xanax, was the 11th-most-prescribed drug in America [in 2003], ahead of top SSRI's such as Zoloft and Paxil. While Alprazolam is not on the U.S. top-20 drug list (it is off-patent and, therefore, cheap), the drug—reckoned by many independent researchers to be among the most addictive in its class—is consumed in massive quantities. Nearly five million people have, at some point, taken Xanax or a similar anti-anxiety medication, for nonmedicinal reasons according to a 2000 survey conducted by the federal Substance Abuse and Mental Health Services Administration.

Drs. Peter Breggin, Fred A. Baughman, Jr., John Breeding, Joyce G. and Iver F. Small, Richard Abrams, and Mary Ann Block are just a tiny few among hundreds of prominent medical professionals now speaking out against the trend of prescribing mood-altering drugs. These defectors maintain that doctors are taking "the easy way out" instead of thoroughly diagnosing and addressing the patient's (or parent's) complaint. They further insist that the practice of mixing SSRI's and benzodiazepines is creating epidemic levels of brain-injured individuals, especially children, whose brains are not yet thoroughly "wired." . . .

Women and Psychiatric Drugs

There are almost twice as many female psychiatric patients as men, and more than half of these are prescribed psychiatric drugs, which they seem more willing to accept. What effect has this had on women?

One outcome has been a vastly decreased sex drive, which frequently becomes permanent even after the drug, or drug cocktail, is stopped. Some 90 percent of women report a lowered libido in as little as eight weeks of starting a course of therapy involving antidepressants such as Prozac, especially in combination with one of the minor tranquilizers. Other side-effects include cessation of menstruation, breast pain, fibrocystic leukorrhea (white or yellow discharge from the vagina), early-onset menopause, menorrhagia (excessive menstrual bleeding), ovarian disorders, spontaneous abortion (sudden loss of a pregnancy), and dyspareunia (painful intercourse).

The news gets worse. An article first published in the *Arizona Republic* was picked up by the *Washington Times* on April 30, 2004, describing a relatively new and growing trend of self-mutilation among teenagers. A Chicago-based self-injury treatment program, Self-Abuse Finally Ends, reports a steady increase in the number of teenagers, mostly girls, who burn, cut, hack and bruise themselves—to *relieve tension*. Cofounder Karen Conterio says another spike occurred during the 2004 school year. Researchers say that the reasons for this vary, including abuse by others, but most self-mutilators "suffer from an underlying psychiatric disorder, such as depression."

Consequently, school personnel nationwide are increasingly pressured to refer girls to psychotherapists, who will give the youngsters antidepressants and tranquilizers. Indeed, it seems that many of the girls had already seen a psychotherapist and either had been, or were taking, psychiatric drugs. Which brings up the old chicken-and-egg question: Did the self-abuse come before or after the drug regimen? And what exactly is so profoundly depressing girls in free societies?

Dr. Armand Nicholi, Jr., a professor at Harvard Medical School of Psychiatry, sees two things: First, the attempt to substitute surrogate mother figures for children via daycare and other arrangements compromises the stability of the child. Then comes the early sexualizing of adolescents that "has led to empty relationships, feelings of self-contempt and worthlessness, an epidemic of venereal disease . . . and a profound sense of loneliness." The latter affects girls more than boys and sets them up for obsessive fear of abandonment in adulthood.

Depression or Exhaustion?

Young or old, women who take tranquilizers and antidepressants are at greater risk than men. So why do adult women willingly take these risks? One answer appears to lie in the obsessions of a sex-and-youth culture that is also beset by feminism. The notion that they can—and, indeed, should—"have it all" has resulted in women feeling defeated, whether they are married with children, "in relationships," or pursuing college and careers. The numerous changes in society, including sexual "freedom," have negatively affected women, contrary to advertisements portraying carefree women using "easy" birth-control patches. In post-1950's America, the cleaning, groceries, and pharmaceuticals are not delivered. The milkman does not leave milk, eggs, and butter. There is no actual human being on the other end of the line when you telephone about a problem. Grocery stores are football-field-sized minimalls. Men put on their socks in the morning and forget about it; women can ruin three pair of pantyhose before lunch.

Much of what passes for depression in women may, in fact, be exhaustion. Except that they can't sleep. They fret over their weight and hair, agonize over every wrinkle, and purchase armloads of beauty products to look as seductive as possible. Then, before turning in, they write up grocery lists, check on the kids' homework, reprogram their cell phones, and iron a blouse—things they cannot do at work. After all that, a woman is wide awake—and not feeling sexy. So she takes one of those "minor tranquilizers."

Research shows that we do not necessarily need to sleep, but we do need to dream. Most psychiatric drugs, including those promoted as sleeping medications, inhibit the critical dream phase of sleep, inducing a state that *looks* like sleep but is merely dreamless and unconscious. Sleep, therefore, is actually impaired or stopped by most psychiatric drugs.

Ironically, many women *want* to perform certain functions, like grocery shopping and caring for children. This was not anticipated when the feminist movement began, and now that females make up half (or more) of the workforce, the results are in: Women on tranqs are overwhelmed by the enormity of their tasks.

Periodical Bibliography

The following articles have been selected to supplement the diverse views presented in this chapter.

B. Bower   "Disorderly Conduct: U.S. Survey Finds High Rates of Mental Illness," *Science News*, June 11, 2005.

Amanda Chesworth   "Tom Cruise, Scientology Bash Psyhiatry; APA Fires Back," *Skeptical Inquirer*, September/October 2005.

Cynthia M.A. Geppert   "Not Enough," *Psychiatric Times*, March 1, 2005.

Michael Jonathan Grinfield   "Celebrity Triggers Tumult over Psychiatric Care: Did the News Media Make Things Worse?" *Psyhiatric Times*, September 1, 2005.

Robert David Jaffee   "Shedding Stigma of the 'Psycho' Straitjacket," *Los Angeles Times*, April 10, 2005.

Diana Mahoney   "Mental Illness Common, Often Goes Untreated," *Internal Medicine News*, August 1, 2005.

Susan McCabe   "Where Is the Mental Health in Psychiatric Mental Health Nursing?" *Perspectives in Psychiatric Care*, July–September 2005.

Steven Pack   "When Does Pleasure Become an Addiction? Treating Everyday Pleasures as Addictions Will Make Victims of Us All," *Nursing Standard*, November 16, 2005.

Marianne Szegedy-Maszak   "Rethinking Abnormal Behavior," *U.S. News & World Report*, May 2, 2005.

Shankar Vedantam   "Prejudice That Debilitates," *Washington Post National Weekly Edition*, December 19–25, 2005.

Kerri Wachter   "Treat Substance Abuse, Mental Illness Together," *Internal Medicine News*, March 15, 2005.

CHAPTER 2

How Should Society Address Mental Illness?

Chapter Preface

In the early 1960s the United States government maintained five hundred thousand hospital beds for the mentally ill in state-run institutions. By the 1970s most of these beds were eliminated, and the occupants of state-run hospitals were transferred to halfway-houses and other temporary community-based institutions. Today, with fewer than seventy thousand spaces available in state institutions, a good number of mentally ill people are homeless and struggling to survive on the streets without therapy or medication.

There are also significant numbers of mentally ill people in jails and prisons. A U.S. Department of Justice Study reports that at least 16 percent of the nation's mentally ill are incarcerated. According to Ed Marciniak, president of the Institute of Urban Life at Loyola University in Chicago, Illinois, "Schizophrenics or manic-depressives are more likely to be arrested for conduct related to their ailments than to be granted refuge in mental health facilities. In New York City, for example, nearly 3,000 mentally ill people are behind bars." Those who are imprisoned and ill seldom receive treatment. Moreover, upon release, they are rarely referred to institutions that could assist them. Many simply become homeless again—then are eventually re-arrested and returned to jail. As Marciniak points out, "Too little is being done to set up . . . halfway homes and detoxification centers or to multiply residences for the troubled mentally ill." The homeless mentally ill are especially vulnerable—a potential danger to themselves and others. This quandary has increased the demand for laws that would facilitate the institutionalization of the mentally ill even when it is against their own will.

While many critics maintain that involuntary commitment is the most pragmatic and compassionate answer to the problem of imprisonment and homelessness among the mentally ill, others caution against forced therapeutic institutionalization. Former psychiatry professor and author Thomas Szasz, for example, believes that involuntary commitment violates the civil rights of mental patients. People who have been labeled as "mentally ill" but who have broken no laws can all too easily end up in an institution where they are forced to submit to psychiatric interventions, including involuntary drugging. Szasz contends that such therapies can do more harm than good, amounting to a de facto imprisonment and punishment of the patient—all in the name of an imprecise yet unchallenged discipline: psychiatry. As Szasz explains,

> If the person called "patient" breaks no law, he has a right to liberty. And if he breaks the law, he ought to be . . . punished in the criminal justice system. It is as simple as that. Nevertheless, so long as conventional wisdom decrees that the mental patient must be protected from himself, that society must be protected from the mental patient, and that both tasks rightfully belong to a psychiatry wielding powers appropriate to the performance of these duties, psychiatric power remains unreformable.

The question of involuntary commitment is an important issue that society must face as it considers the plight of the mentally ill. Most mentally ill people, however, are not criminally dangerous—many live, work, and form relationships in the ordinary world. The following chapter further examines the dilemma of involuntary commitment as well as other issues related to how society should deal with the mentally ill.

> "When [the mentally ill] are thoroughly uncontrolled, we must do something to them to protect both themselves and the rest of us in their midst."

The Mentally Ill Often Need Involuntary Psychiatric Treatment

Kenneth Richard Fox

In the following viewpoint Kenneth Richard Fox recounts his experience of living with a wife who had bipolar disorder, formerly known as manic depression. Her illness did not become apparent until they had been married several years, when she began to exhibit symptoms of clinical depression. Although she consulted several psychiatrists, she became delusional, violent, and suicidal as her illness intensified. Because it is difficult to commit someone for involuntary therapy or hospitalization, Fox was unable to procure better treatment for her. He concludes that doctors, courts, and social service networks must become more assertive in helping the severely mentally ill—even if it is against their will. Fox is the CEO of Trans/Global Technology, a medical research and development company.

Kenneth Richard Fox, "Monster in Our Midst: Living with Bipolar Disorder," *World and I*, vol. 19, no. 2, February 2004, pp. 251–259. Copyright 2004 News World Communications, Inc. Reproduced by permission.

As you read, consider the following questions:

1. When a therapist would suggest to Fox's wife that she should try hospitalization or electric shock, how would she respond?

2. According to Fox, how did Wendy's symptoms change as her depression deepened into bipolar disorder?

3. What was the incident that ended the author's marriage?

I was driving about 35 miles per hour when, out of the corner of my right eye, I saw a shiny reflection coming directly toward my chest, I grabbed for the forearm and stopped the blade just inches away. My other hand grasped the steering wheel, barely keeping the car from going into a ravine, while my right foot hit the brake. . . .

Wendy and I had met ten years earlier, near the end of my medical residency, and there were times that I thought it had been a match made in heaven. David, our second child, had just arrived when the first signs of Wendy's illness appeared. Our eldest, Kim, was just over three, and the four of us seemed to be the perfect family. Kim was fantastic, and I expected little less from David. I was an eye surgeon and Wendy a speech pathologist. We were, I thought, well established in the community with a nice circle of friends.

Wendy had always been full of energy, positive and forward-looking, highly social, very solid, and responsible. People came to know her for these qualities, and I felt very lucky to have her as my wife and best friend.

The Beginning of Trouble

In the early days after David's birth, Wendy was understandably not quite the same as before; she had two handfuls of responsibility. She began to cancel some professional appointments. Wendy had also been very active in a number of organizations, and, in time, some of that slowed, too.

I was working long hours, so it wasn't until David's first birthday that I realized my wife had developed a habit of sleeping in and leaving his morning care to our live-in nanny. Wendy, who used to insist on doing everything herself, was doing a lot less. She was tired and short-tempered but insisted nothing was wrong. She had a physical examination, and her doctor said she was in good shape.

A couple of years passed. Wendy was still tired and irritable, and she often couldn't sleep through the night. She started seeing psychiatrists. She was diagnosed with severe depression, which may have been triggered by our son's birth. Most of her doctors were reluctant to tell me any more than that because I was the spouse, not the patient, even though I was a professional colleague. Something significant was intruding into our lives, separating us and dividing the family, and her doctors were throwing a cloak of professional silence over it.

The Darkness of Depression

Wendy went through about ten psychiatrists that I knew about. She stopped filing insurance claims, so I had no way to know who she was seeing or any further diagnosis. She was secretive about what her medication was and whether she was taking it. If she was on medication, I couldn't tell the difference. She fluctuated between denying that anything was wrong and being overwhelmed by shame about her problem. When a psychiatrist proposed electroshock therapy or hospitalization, she'd stop seeing him only to find another, searching for one who would tell her that she was okay.

Her father, it turned out, had suffered from major depression, caused by a chemical imbalance in the brain, before he descended into manic depression. This disease, also known as bipolar disorder, tosses the sufferer between extreme highs and lows. Wendy's father died when she was a teenager. She had told me he died of a heart attack, but I later found out he had committed suicide and her family had moved away in part because they felt disgraced.

Bipolar Disorder

Descriptions offered by people with bipolar disorder give valuable insights into the various mood states associated with the illness:

Depression: I doubt completely my ability to do anything well. It seems as though my mind has slowed down and burned out to the point of being virtually useless. . . . [I am] haunt[ed] . . . with the total, the desperate hopelessness of it all. . . .

Hypomania: At first when I'm high, it's tremendous . . . ideas are fast . . . like shooting stars you follow until brighter ones appear. . . . All shyness disappears, the right words and gestures are suddenly there . . . uninteresting people, things become intensely interesting. . . . Your marrow is infused with unbelievable feelings of ease, power, well-being, omnipotence, euphoria. . . .

Mania: The fast ideas become too fast and there are far too many. . . . Overwhelming confusion replaces clarity. . . . Infectious humor ceases to amuse. Your friends become frightened. . . . Everything is now against the grain . . . you are irritable, angry, frightened, uncontrollable, and trapped.

Melissa Spearing, "Bipolar Disorder,"
National Institute of Mental Health, February 17, 2006.
www.nimh.nih.gov.

He used to beat her and perhaps her older sister, Sharon, who also suffered from major depression. Wendy would never admit any of this; from what I was able to understand, she never discussed these issues with her psychiatrists.

Her greatest fear was of becoming "like her father." Her other fear was that she would lose her children. The time came when she sometimes no longer knew what was real. As her depression deepened into manic depression, my wife had become just like her father.

A Suicide Attempt

A few of the doctors who didn't mind discussing the problem with me said they had urged Wendy to tell the children, and that she and no one else had to tell them. The point of this had not only to do with her parenting but also her inheritance of this disease. But she never did. She was afraid that if they or anyone else knew, she might lose her family and then even kill herself.

Wendy tried to commit suicide at least once by taking an overdose of pills. I came home from work late one night and found her befuddled and nearly unconscious. I believe if I had not been there, she might not have made it through the night.

Though I was a doctor, there was pitifully little I could do to help my wife, our children, and myself. All of us were suffering.

When she descended into manic depression, Wendy became at times paranoid and delusional and didn't trust anyone. She projected things she thought or did onto other people. As the person closest to her, I became her prime target.

Emotional Seesaw

She was a monolith of anger. In the major depression years, she turned her anger against herself. In the bipolar years, she heaped her anger on others, mostly on those nearest to her.

She accused me and other people of trying to alienate our children from her, steal her money, damage her speech therapy practice, destroy her friendships, drive her crazy, hurt her, and ruin her reputation. Everyone was out to get her.

By the time David was four, Wendy was much less able to work or care for the children. I sold my medical practice shortly thereafter to devote more of my time to this crisis and to taking care of my family. I didn't know what else to do.

I joined a support group for spouses and other family members of manic-depressives and started seeing a therapist, one whom Wendy and I had gone to early on and she had discarded. I wasn't alone anymore; there were others who understood the depth of my despair in this situation. I began to appreciate and understand that others suffer with this same problem all too often.

I began the long, slow process of emerging from "codependence," living the same anguished existence as the partner-patient, like being stuck in the same box with her. The codependent partner needs to break out to stay healthy. I sought to regain my own self-confidence. It was a slow and difficult process. In time, I started to see things more clearly.

After six years of illness, my wife suddenly went into remission. We were able to love again, and life seemed wonderful once more. I began then to think that the manic depression had cured itself.

A year later, the seesaw tipped the other way. The relapse into full-blown bipolar disorder came hard and fast. In the manic phase, Wendy felt better; the black hole of despair went away. There was no stopping her. She was on the move. She got things done. But she was a raving lunatic, which became increasingly apparent to just about everyone she knew. Most of our friends became somewhat more distant. The relatively few friendships that withstood the test of that long period were sweet, indeed, and helped me a lot.

The family therapist we went to at that time threw up his hands, unable to deal with Wendy's anger and abuse. She also had run-ins with authority figures. Wendy crushed anything that got in the way of her systematic denial.

To treat the mania is to risk the return of the depression, a kind of over-correction. No one in his "wrong mind" would want to do that. Behavior during mania is laced with uncontrollable and dangerous excesses that may include violence, hypersexual activity, insomnia, overworking, overspending, or other extreme behaviors. Manic-depressives often seem normal to people they meet casually. For those who see more of them, the problem is usually unmistakable.

A Prisoner of the Mind

However bad or daunting the major depression had been for me and the children, this mania seemed a hundred times worse. Wendy vented her anger through violence, most often against me but sometimes against our son and other people. In her delusions she believed that almost everyone around her was evil or potentially harmful to her.

After shedding so many psychiatrists along the way, she eventually found a quack psychotherapist who seemed perfectly satisfied to see her for about ten minutes once a month and ask if she was okay. Of course, to herself, she was just fine. This pseudosupport kept her going for a while. He was a far cry from the psychiatrists who wanted to hospitalize her and start major drug or even electroshock therapy. She felt encouraged. The trouble was, this "treatment" was encouraging the monster that was destroying the wife I loved. It is the oddest feeling when this kind of mental illness, this intangible and overpowering force, comes between you and someone you love dearly.

I spent about eleven years in all trying to deal with one phase of her illness or another and seeing our children suffer because of it. When they grew older, she would sometimes tell Kim or even David that she was just "a little down."

Wendy was a prisoner of her brain chemistry. Our kids lived in a house of horrors for much of their formative years and may also have inherited the propensity for the disease from their mother. I was married to the monster that had taken over my wife and my children's mother.

In the last two years of our hellish relationship, my wife physically assaulted me no fewer than twenty-five times. I wound up bruised, scalded, and cut just about every few weeks. These unprovoked attacks even sometimes occurred when I was sleeping. I reported each episode to the police, who wanted to arrest my wife. I refused. I didn't see the criminal justice system as a solution; I didn't see my wife as a criminal but as someone who was very sick. A female police officer who responded to one of my calls told me that her male policeman partner had also been the victim of a petite but physically abusive wife with apparently a very similar illness who wound up in jail.

The twenty-sixth and final violent episode was an apparently premeditated attempt on my life, with a kitchen knife, while I was driving. That was the blow that ultimately ended our marriage. I had to save myself, but I couldn't help her or the children.

No Safety Net

I blame my medical colleagues and those in the other helping professions in part for not being aggressive enough about diagnosing, investigating, and treating this type of mental illness, especially in potentially dangerous cases such as this one was. True, doctors are bound by the patient privilege doctrine, but they are at the same time sometimes the only ones privy to the potential public safety menace that certain of these more violent patients represent. Just as psychiatrists should act to attempt to prevent a suicide, there must be a mechanism for them to suggest to some authority the violent tendencies of certain patients they may see. Only in this manner can these patients be protected from their own destruction or from harming others. In Wendy's case, her extreme denial and the fact that she frequently would change psychiatrists were severe confounding factors in both providing her with more and better treatment and in protecting those around her. However, the level of awareness of psychiatrists in contact professionally with these types of patients must remain very high so that they may see through that cloudy veil worn by patients in denial.

The public "safety net"—police, courts, and social welfare agencies—is also often most unhelpful. Although my own initial reticence to bring my wife into the criminal justice system in the face of her repeated violent episodes was probably not helpful in the long run, once it became quite apparent that there was something drastically wrong, things did not get any better. The U.S. Attorney's office charged with prosecuting Wendy was ultimately cajoled into dismissing the serious assault charge against her because the specter of trying her and in the process interjecting our two children even more into the middle of what was a very ugly situation was highly unappealing.

Taking a singleminded and thoroughly unenlightened view of all of this, the divorce court simply ignored Wendy's significant mental health history, unwilling to require an independent medical evaluation that might have led to an attempt to moderate or modify her violent behavior. That might well have ultimately led to her hospitalization for a trial of medicines or other therapy such as electric shock treatment. That court also was unable to bring itself to separate the potentially dangerous mother from her minor children until sufficient medical remediation of the condition had been accomplished. By allowing the severe adverse effects of a pathologically angry and violent mother to persist in the home, her two minor children left in contact with her, the children were doomed to suffer long-standing adverse psychological effects. The system makes it virtually impossible to privately bring an action to involuntarily commit these types of individuals. Generally, several psychiatrists have to testify that they have personally seen solid evidence of the worst of the violent behavior; given the denial, the lack of compliance, and proper follow-up in this instance and in others like it this standard is most unlikely to often be met.

Society Must Do More

I feel strongly that we must do much more for people with severe depression and/or bipolar disorder. When they are thoroughly uncontrolled, we must do something to them to protect both themselves and the rest of us in their midst. Year by year we learn more about this common but sometimes violent disorder and the havoc that it visits upon individuals, families, and society. Doctors involved in treating these patients need to be as proactive as possible. Judges ought to be further educated about the horrible potential consequences of this condition; the law must generously require them to act in the best interests of minor children but also protect those patients and loved ones around them from the ravages of this disease. The police need to understand more about bipolar disorder and its many faces; social service networks that interface with these people also should act in a more inspired and proactive fashion in their dealings with them.

| *"There is no scientific basis whatever for preventive psychiatric detention, also known as involuntary mental hospitalisation or civil commitment."*

Involuntary Psychiatric Treatment Is Unethical

Thomas Szasz

Involuntary psychiatric treatment violates the moral foundations of English and American law, argues Thomas Szasz in the following viewpoint. All too often, those who exhibit disturbing behaviors are labeled as "mentally ill" by psychiatrists, Szasz points out. This enables the state to commit the offending person to a mental hospital, which in the author's opinion is just another form of incarceration. Mental patients are thus stripped of their civil rights and subjected to forced drugging and other unwanted treatments. No law-abiding citizen should be deprived of his or her freedoms simply because a doctor labeled him or her as dangerous, asserts Szasz. Szasz, author of The Myth of Mental Illness *and* Psychiatric Slavery, *formerly taught psychiatry as the State University of New York.*

Thomas Szasz, "Psychiatry and the Control of Dangerousness: On the Apotropaic Function of the Term 'Mental Illness,'" *Journal of Social Work Education*, vol. 39, no. 3, Fall 2003, pp. 375–81. Copyright 2003 Council on Social Work Education. Reproduced by permission of *Journal of Social Work Education* and Penguin Putnam Inc.

As you read, consider the following questions:

1. What is an apotropaic word, according to Szasz?
2. What is the author's opinion on suicide?
3. In Szasz's opinion, why do conservatives tend to agree with liberals about use of coercive tactics in treating mental health problems?

Life is full of dangers. Our highly developed consciousness makes us, of all living forms in the universe, the most keenly aware of, and the most adept at protecting ourselves from, dangers. Magic and religion are mankind's earliest warning systems. Science arrived on the scene only about 400 years ago, and scientific medicine only 200 years ago. Some time ago I suggested that "formerly, when religion was strong and science weak, men mistook magic for medicine; now, when science is strong and religion weak, men mistake medicine for magic." [1]

We flatter and deceive ourselves if we believe that we have outgrown the apotropaic use of language (from the Greek *apostropaios* meaning "to turn away").

Many people derive comfort from magical objects (amulets), and virtually everyone finds reassurance in magical words (incantations). The classic example of an apotropaic is the word "abracadabra," which the *American Heritage Dictionary of the English Language* defines as "a magical charm or incantation having the power to ward off disease of disaster." In the ancient world, abracadabra was a magic word, the letters of which were arranged in an inverted pyramid and worn as an amulet around the neck to protect the wearer against disease or trouble. One fewer letter appeared in each line of the pyramid until only the letter "a" remained to form the vertex of the triangle. As the letters disappeared, so supposedly did the disease or trouble.

I submit that we use phrases like "dangerousness to self and others" and "psychiatric treatment" as apotropaics to ward off dangers we fear, much as ancient magicians warded off the dangers people feared by means of incantations, exemplified by "abracadabra." Growing reliance on compulsory mental health interventions for protection against crime and suicide illustrate the phenomenon. Physicians, criminologists, politicians, and the public use advances in medicine and neuroscience to convince themselves that such interventions are "scientific" and do not violate the moral and legal foundations of English and American law. This is a serious error. There is no scientific basis whatever for preventive psychiatric detention, also known as involuntary mental hospitalisation or civil commitment. And the procedure is a patent violation of due process and the presumption of innocence.

We call all manner of human problems "(mental) diseases," and convince ourselves that drugs and conversation (therapy) solve such problems. Solutions exist, however, only for mathematical problems and some medical problems. For human problems, there are no solutions. Conflict, disagreement, unhappiness, the proverbial slings and arrows of outrageous fortune are challenges that we must cope with, not solve. Only after we admit that our solutions are illusions can we begin to develop more rational and more humane methods for dealing with "mental illness" and the "dangerous mental patient."

We are proud that we do not punish acts or beliefs that upset others, but do not injure them and hence do not constitute crimes. Yet, we punish people—albeit we call it "treatment"—for annoying family members (and others) with behaviours they deem "dangerous" and also for "being suicidal." To be sure, persons who exhibit such behaviors—labeled "schizophrenics," "persons with dangerous severe personality disorders," and "suicidal patients"—frighten others, especially those who must associate with them. Unable to control noncriminal "offences" by means of criminal law sanctions, how can the offended persons and society protect themselves from their unwanted fellow men and women?

One way is by "divorcing" them. However, this method of separating oneself from an unwanted companion—especially when it involves relations between disturbing and disturbed spouses or between disturbing adult children and their disturbed parents—strikes most people as an unacceptable rejection of family obligation. Psychiatrists offer to relieve the disturbed person of the burden of coping with his disturbed relative by incarcerating the latter and calling it "care" and "treatment."

How do psychiatrists do this? By allying themselves with the coercive apparatus of the state and declaring the offending individual mentally ill and dangerous to him- or herself or others. This magic mantra allows us to incarcerate him in a prison we call a "mental hospital." Ostensibly, the term "mental illness" (or "psychopathology") names a pathological condition of disease, similar, say, to diabetes; actually, it names a social tactic or justification, permitting family members, courts, and society as a body, to separate themselves from individuals who exhibit, or are claimed to exhibit, certain behaviours identified as "dangerous mental illnesses." This tactic is dramatically illustrated by the following "advice" appearing on the Web site of the National Alliance for the Mentally Ill (NAMI), a mental health advocacy organisation that identifies itself as representing "more than 200,000 families, consumers, and providers across the country." As will be evident, NAMI represents the interests of mental patients the same way that the Ku Klux Klan represented the interests of black Americans.

> Sometime, during the course of your loved one's illness, you may need the police. By preparing now, before you need help, you can make the day you need help go much more smoothly. . . . It is often difficult to get 911 to respond to your calls if you need someone to come & take your MI

[mentally ill] relation to a hospital emergency room (ER). They may not believe that you really need help. And if they do send the police, the police are often reluctant to take someone for involuntary commitment. That is because cops are concerned about liability. . . . When calling 911, the best way to get quick action is to say, "Violent EDP," or "Suicidal EDP." EDP stands for Emotionally Disturbed Person. This shows the operator that you know what you're talking about. Describe the danger very specifically. "He's a danger to himself" is not as good as "This morning my son said he was going to jump off the roof." . . . Also, give past history of violence. This is especially important if the person is not acting up. . . . When the police come, they need compelling evidence that the person is a danger to self or others before they can involuntarily take him or her to the ER for evaluation. . . . While AMI / FAMI [Alliance for the Mentally Ill/Florida Alliance for the Mentally Ill] is not suggesting you do this, the fact is that some families have learned to "turn over the furniture" before calling the police.[2]

Giving false information to the police is a crime, unless it is in the cause of "mental health."

In the United Kingdom, unlike in the United States, there still are physicians, psychiatrists, and medical journals that view these developments with concern, if not alarm. The publication of a United Kingdom government white paper for a new mental health act, in 2000, that would provide for the psychiatric detention of persons diagnosed as having a "dangerous severe personality disorder" has duly alarmed some doctors in Britain.[3-5] I am afraid, however, that their lamentations are too feeble, and come too late.

The Danger of the Concept of "Dangerousness"

In *The Myth of Mental Illness*, I showed that the idea of mental illness implies dangerousness and thus requires and justifies psychiatric coercions.[6] To civilly commit a person, a psychiatrist (or physician) must certify that the subject suffers from a mental illness and is dangerous to himself and/or others. It is not by accident that when psychiatry was a young and marginalised medical specialty, its primary social function was controlling persons dangerous to others ("mad"); and that now, when it is a mature and respected medical specialty, its primary function is controlling persons who are dangerous to themselves ("suicide risks").

In his classic treatise on schizophrenia, Eugen Bleuler complained: "People are being forced to continue to live a life that has become unbearable for them for valid reasons.... Even if a few more [patients] killed themselves, does this reason justify the fact that we torture hundreds of patients and aggravate their disease?" [7]

Why are psychiatrists expected to prevent suicide by depriving the "suspect" of liberty? The idea of suicide makes us nervous. We cannot decide whether killing oneself is a "right" or a wrong, an element of our inalienable personal liberty or an offence of some sort that ought to be prohibited and perhaps punished. We are too uptight about suicide to recognize that killing oneself is sometimes a reasonable and right thing to do, sometimes an unreasonable and wrong thing to do, but that, in either case, it ought to be treated as an act that falls outside the scope of interference by the state.[8]

The right to kill oneself is the supreme symbol of personal autonomy. Formerly, the church allied with the state prohibited and punished the act. Now, psychiatry, as an arm of the state, prohibits the act and "treats" it as if it were a symptom of an underlying disease (typically, depression or schizophrenia). The deprivation of liberty intrinsic to such an intervention is viewed not as a human rights violation but as a human rights protection. The modern reader may be surprised, perhaps even shocked, at seeing the words "prohibition" and "suicide" bracketed. Lack of familiarity with the long history of the religious prohibition against self murder, together with unquestioning acceptance of coercive psychiatric suicide prevention as "therapy," make such a reaction a virtual certainty. This is unfortunate.

Formerly, religious doctrine defined the permissible uses of the body. Its impermissible uses—self abuse (masturbation), sex abuse (homosexuality and other "perversions"), substance abuse (drunkenness and gluttony), and self murder (suicide)— were sins, crimes, or both, punished by informal or formal sanctions. Substituting medical for religious doctrine, the modern state, in collaboration with psychiatry, transformed each of these behaviours into diseases of the mind, a view that prevailed through most of the nineteenth and twentieth centuries. After the second world war, and more rapidly in recent decades, some of these mental maladies were divested of their disease status. In my own lifetime, masturbation ceased to be a mental disease, or a cause of disease, and homosexuality became not just normal but a "right" others were legally obligated to respect. Yet, during the same period, political, psychiatric, and popular condemnation of self medication and self killing intensified. Using substances decreed to be "dangerous" and illegal is now viewed as an "international plague," justifying a worldwide "war on drugs." [9] Rejecting life and wanting to kill oneself is defined as a severe mental illness characterized by "dangerousness to self," and is treated as a quasicrime with coercions called "treatments" (especially involuntary "hospitalisation" and forced drugging). Success in committing suicide is regarded as a "waste," a preventable medical tragedy, often attributed to medical negligence.[10]

It is a fundamental principle of English and American law that only persons charged with and convicted of certain crimes are subject to imprisonment. Persons who respect other peoples' rights to life, liberty, and property have an inalienable right to their own life, liberty, and property. Having a disposition or propensity to break the law is not a crime.

Serious debate about matters regarded as mental health problems, especially suicide, is taboo. Liberals have a love affair with coercion in the name of mental health. Conservatives—fearful lest they be dismissed as not compassionate enough about the mentally ill and not scientific enough about mental illness—join in the celebration of psychiatric statism. A columnist for the conservative magazine *National Review* agrees with the psychiatric dogma that "it is mental illness that causes most suicides: depression, manic depression, and schizophrenia. . . . The conservative critique of the therapeutic culture," he warns, "will not get a hearing until conservatives face up to the reality of mental illness." [11]

Speaking about, much less supporting, a right to suicide strikes most people as unimaginably uncompassionate. This opinion is the result of viewing suicide as caused by depression, and depression as a kind of unnecessary, curable unhappiness. We regard this perspective as enlightened and scientific, when in fact it is naive and conceited. Toward the end of *Brave New World*—a scientistic dystopia in which all conflicts and discomforts have been eliminated—the human remnant [the book's author, Aldous] Huxley calls the Savage, and his opponent, the "Controller" Mustapha Mond, engage in the following dialogue:

> . . . "We prefer to do things comfortably" [said the Controller].
>
> "But I don't want comfort. I want God, I want poetry, I want real danger, I want freedom, I want goodness, I want sin."
>
> "In fact," said Mustapha Mond, "you're claiming the right to be unhappy."
>
> "All right, then," said the Savage defiantly, "I'm claiming the right to be unhappy." [12]

For the person who kills himself, suicide may be the realisation of diverse aspirations and expectations. For society, suicide is, first and foremost, an act of *lese majeste* (literally, "injured majesty"). *Webster's Dictionary* defines the term as "an offense violating the dignity of a ruler as the representative of a sovereign power; detraction from the dignity or importance of a constituted authority."

For millennia, suicide was *lese majeste* against the church/ state, the supreme representation of legitimate authority for people who worship a god and want a good life in the hereafter. Today, suicide is *lese majeste* against the Therapeutic State, the supreme representation of legitimate authority for people who worship health and want to stay alive as long as possible.

Regarding the issue of "dangerousness to others" as a quasicrime—once we cease to regard "it" as a "condition caused by mental illness"—there is not much to say.

In the current climate of opinion, however, things are no longer that simple. People fear, often for good reasons, persons not susceptible under our legal system for detention in prison. Persons called "sex offenders" are the most widely publicised offenders who fall into this class. In 1997, in *Kansas v Leroy Hendricks*, the US Supreme Court declared: "States have a right to use psychiatric hospitals to confine certain sex offenders once they have completed their prison terms, even if those offenders do not meet mental illness commitment criteria." [13] In February 2000, Wisconsin's oldest prison inmate, a 95 year old man, was "resentenced" as a sexual predator, after a psychologist "testified . . . [that] psychological tests performed on Ellefson indicated if he was given a chance, he would commit a [sex] crime. . . . After only minutes of deliberation, the jury found that Ellef J Ellefson should be committed for mental treatment under the sexual predator law." [14]

As I noted, the practice of preventive psychiatric detention has not gone unremarked by British commentators. John J Sandford, a British forensic psychiatrist complained: "'The preventive detention of those with untreatable mental disorders is already widely practised in England. Under the Mental

Health Act (1983) people ... [are] detained indefinitely in hospital regardless of response to treatment and on grounds of risk to self as well as others. Secure and open psychiatric hospitals are full of such patients." [15] This view was echoed in an editorial in the *British Medical Journal*: "The growing pressures on them [psychiatrists] to deliver public protection was perhaps inevitable, given the rise of biopsychomedical paradigms as explanations for the vicissitudes of life in modern Western society. Psychiatrists have played their part by assuming the authority to explain, categorise, manage, and prognose in situations where well defined disease (arguably their only clear cut remit) was not present." [16]

Psychiatry is part law and part medicine. It is the psychiatrist's social mandate to function as a double agent: that is, to help voluntary patients cope with their problems in living and to help relatives and society rid themselves of certain unwanted persons, under medical auspices. The latter task requires coercing the denominated patient; the former is rendered impossible by the slightest threat of coercion, much less its actual exercise. The psychiatrist's mandate violates Jesus' injunction, "Render therefore unto Caesar the things which are Caesar's; and unto God the things that are God's."[17]

True psychiatric reform is contingent on separating the psychiatrist's two, mutually incompatible roles and functions.

References

1. Szasz, T.S., *The Second Sin*. Garden City, NY: Doubleday, 1974, p. 128.
2. Jaffe, D.J., "How to Prepare for an Emergency," www.nami.org.
3. Buchanan, A. and Leese, M., "Detention of People with Dangerous Severe Personality Disorders: A Systematic Review," *Lancet*, vol. 358, pp. 1955–59
4. Farnham, F.R. and James, D.V., "Dangerousness and Dangerous Law," *Lancet*, vol. 358, p. 1926.
5. White, S.M., "Preventive Detention Must Be Resisted by the Medical Profession," *Journal of Medical Ethics*, vol. 28, pp. 95–108.
6. Szasz, T.S., *The Myth of Mental Illness*. New York: HarperCollins, 1974 (first published 1961).
7. Bleuler, E., *Dementia Praecox or the Group of Schizophrenias*. New York: International Universities Press, 1950 pp. 488–89 (first published 1911).

8. Szasz, T.S., *Fatal Freedom: The Ethics and Politics of Suicide*. Westport, CT: Praeger, 1999.
9. Szasz, T.S., *Our Right to Drugs: The Case for a Free Market*. Syracuse: Syracuse University Press, 1996 (first published 1992).
10. Anonymous, "Such a Waste" [editorial], *Economist*, December 8, 2001, www.ncpa.org.
11. Ponnuru, R., "Inner Darkness," *National Review*, April 3, 2000, p. 48.
12. Huxley, A., *Brave New World*. New York: HarperPerennial, 1969, p. 246 (first published in 1932).
13. *Kansas v. Leroy Hendricks*, 117 S. Ct. 2072, excerpts from opinions on status of sex offenders, from *New York Times*, June 24, 1997, p. B11.
14. Associated Press, "Jury: 95-Year-Old Sexual Predator Is Still a Threat," *Syracuse Herald-Journal*, February 2, 2000, p. A8.
15. Sandford, J.J., Public Health Psychiatry and Crime Prevention, *BMJ*, vol. 318, p. 1354.
16. Anonymous, [editorial], *BMJ*, vol. 318.
17. Holy Bible, Matthew xxii, 21.

> "It is now time to take the next step and provide effective treatment to distressed [veterans]."

Mentally Ill Veterans Need More Effective Psychotherapy

Patrice G.W. Norton

Soldiers returning from combat need more effective treatments for war-related psychiatric disorders, contends Patrice G.W. Norton in the following viewpoint. According to surveys, a growing percentage of U.S. troops are experiencing depression and post-traumatic stress disorder (PTSD), but they are often worried that seeking therapy will stigmatize them, Norton reports. Distressed soldiers need improved access to treatment as well as assurances that their mental health problems will be kept confidential. Norton is a contributing writer to Clinical Psychiatry News.

As you read, consider the following questions:

1. According to Charles Hoge, as quoted by the author, how could mentally ill soldiers' fear of stigmatization be reduced?

Patrice G.W. Norton, "Soldiers' Mental Health Needs Are Not Being Met," *Clinical Psychiatry News*, vol. 32, no. 8, August 2004, pp. 1–2. Copyright 2004 International Medical News Group. Reproduced by permission.

2. What percentage of U.S. soldiers returning from duty in Iraq were found to have mental health problems, according to Norton?

3. What increases the prevalence of PTSD among combat troops, according to Norton?

The first study of the mental health of U.S. troops who fought in Iraq and Afghanistan found about one in six reported experiencing a mental health problem and one in eight reported symptoms of post-traumatic stress disorder.

Of those whose responses were positive for a mental disorder, only 23%–40% reported receiving professional help—mostly because of concerns about being stigmatized.

Subjects whose responses were positive for a mental disorder were twice as likely as were those whose responses were negative to report concerns about possible stigmatization and other barriers to seeking mental health services, the study found.

More Services Are Needed

"This finding has immediate public health implications," reported Dr. Charles W. Hoge of the department of psychiatry and behavioral sciences at the Walter Reed Army Institute of Research in Silver Spring, Md.

Dr. Hoge suggested that the perception of stigmatization and other barriers could be reduced through education, and by providing more mental health services in primary care clinics and confidential counseling through employee assistance programs.

Screening for major depression, which is done in military primary care settings, also should be expanded to include screening for post-traumatic stress disorder (PTSD).

An accompanying editorial noted that military personnel are skeptical that the use of mental health services can remain confidential.

Perceived Barriers to Seeking Mental Health Services

	Surveyed Troops Who Met Criteria for a Mental Disorder	Surveyed Troops Who Did Not Meet Criteria for a Mental Disorder
I would be seen as weak.	65%	31%
My unit leaders might treat me differently.	63%	33%
Members of my unit might have less confidence in me.	59%	31%
There would be difficulty getting time off work for treatment.	55%	22%
My leaders would blame me for the problem.	51%	20%
It would harm my career.	50%	24%

New England Journal of Medicine, *vol. 351, no. 1, 2004.*

Troops were able to acknowledge PTSD-related problems in an anonymous survey, but "they apparently were afraid to seek assistance for fear that a scarlet P could doom their careers," wrote Dr. Matthew J. Friedman, executive director of the Department of Veterans Affairs' National Center for Post-Traumatic Stress Disorder.

Combat Experience and Mental Illness

A total of 6,201 members of four U.S. combat infantry units—three Army units and one Marine Corps unit—were given an anonymous survey either before their deployment to Iraq or

3–4 months after their return from combat duty in Iraq or Afghanistan. The outcomes included major depression, generalized anxiety, and PTSD, which were evaluated on the basis of standardized, self-administered screening instruments.

The percentage of subjects whose responses met the screening criteria for major depression, generalized anxiety, or PTSD was significantly higher after duty in Iraq (15.6%–17.1%) than after duty in Afghanistan (11.2%) or before deployment to Iraq (9.3%).

The largest difference was in the rate of PTSD, which was between 12.2% and 12.6% after duty in Iraq vs. 6.2% after duty in Afghanistan, and 5.0% before deployment to Iraq.

For all groups responding after deployment, there was a strong reported relation between the prevalence of PTSD and combat experience such as being shot at, handling dead bodies, knowing someone who was killed, or killing enemy combatants.

The prevalence of PTSD increased in a linear manner with the number of firefights during deployment: 4.5% for no firefights, 9.3% for one to two firefights, 12.7% for three to five firefights, and 19.3% for more than five firefights.

The Army's estimates of PTSD may be conservative, partly because it is too early to assess the magnitude of the mental health problems related to deployment, Dr. Friedman wrote. Based on previous findings, the prevalence of PTSD might rise considerably during the 2 years after veterans return from combat duty, and psychiatric disorders might increase as a result of the war becoming an armed conflict that is ongoing.

Long-Term Illnesses Could Increase

PTSD could increase in the coming years among these veterans, agreed Dr. Sandro Galea, who recently completed studies of New York City residents that found a spike in reported PTSD 2 years after the terrorist attacks of Sept. 11, 2001. The data also suggest that there are different determinants of people who get PTSD and those who keep it in the long run, Dr. Galea told [*Clinical Psychiatry News*].

"Our work suggests that the course of PTSD in the long term is complicated and that ongoing traumatic experiences may be associated with long-term symptoms and associated disability," said Dr. Galea of the Center for Urban Epidemiologic Studies, New York Academy of Medicine.

Dr. Friedman called the report "unprecedented," noting that it is the first time there has been such an early assessment of the prevalence of war-related psychiatric disorders reported, while the fighting continues. There are predeployment data, and data showing that the perception of stigmatization has the power to deter troops from seeking help even when they recognize the severity of their psychiatric problems.

"Our acknowledgment of the psychiatric costs of war has promoted the establishment of better methods of detecting and treating war-related psychiatric disorders," he said. "It is now time to take the next step and provide effective treatment to distressed men and women, along with credible safeguards of confidentiality."

> "Although therapists clearly help some soldiers, there is only so much emotional damage from war they can fix."

Psychotherapy May Not Benefit Military Veterans

Paula J. Caplan

In the following viewpoint Paula J. Caplan maintains that psychotherapy may not be adequate to deal with the problems of military veterans. The military's approach to therapy is to offer brief counseling or psychiatric drugs for traumatized soldiers, who then get sent into battle again. This is cruel, Caplan argues, because the deep problems these troops are encountering will simply resurface later. Furthermore, a soldier's emotional response to the horrors of war is usually a normal human reaction to disturbing realities—not a sign of mental illness. Therapy may help some soldiers, but what they really need is for citizens to hear their stories and recognize the devastating consequences of war, the author concludes. Caplan is a spokeswoman for the Association of Women in Psychology.

As you read, consider the following questions:

1. What is the suicide rate for American soldiers in Iraq, according to the U.S. Army?

Paula J. Caplan, "Too Little, Too Late?" *Washington Post National Weekly Edition*, vol. 21, no. 47, September 13–19, 2004, p. 23. Reproduced by permission of the author.

2. What is a typical soldier's initial response to the horrors of war, according to the author?

3. In Caplan's opinion, what is misguided about the debriefings that the military gives to soldiers returning home?

In 1996, in his late twenties, Robert joined the Army Reserve to get help with college tuition. The reserve's demands weren't much of a hardship—until [the terrorist attacks of September 11, 2001], when his life was turned upside down. First assigned to full-time duty as an airport guard, he was sent to Kabul eight months later. In Afghanistan, he counted the minutes until he could get back home. But when he did, half a year later, he found himself "all at sea." The people around him, he felt, "acted like I'd never left. For them, nothing was different." His feelings of turmoil were exacerbated by an uneasy sense that he had no right to them, as his unit had been shot at only once.

When he couldn't shake feelings of depression after nearly a year at home, his sister finally suggested that he see a therapist. It seemed like the obvious solution to her, and I can see why. After all, we sent many Vietnam and Gulf War vets behind psychotherapists' doors to deal with their anguish, and we've come to think it's the best thing to do. Unfortunately, in our over-psychologized society, we've also come to think that it's the only thing to do.

We've failed to learn what the vets of previous wars have taught us—that although therapists clearly help some soldiers, there is only so much emotional damage from war they can fix. Leaving this work to psychotherapists alone may be not only harmful to the soldiers but also dangerous for us as a nation, because it helps hide the consequences of combat, making it easier for us to go to war again the next time.

Simply sending frightened, angry soldiers off to therapists conveys disturbing messages: that we don't want to listen, that we're afraid we're not qualified to listen, and that they should talk to someone who gets paid to listen. The implication is that their devastation is abnormal, that it is a mental illness, and this only adds to their burdens. Yet since there's intense debate even among experts about the definition of mental illness, it's all the more important for the rest of us to let returnees know that we don't consider them weak or crazy for having problems.

Reactions to the Horrors of War

According to U.S. Army reports, the suicide rate for American soldiers in Iraq is 17.3 per 100,000, nearly five times the rate for the Gulf War and 11 percent higher than for Vietnam. . . . Clearly, the emotional casualties of this war are already extremely high, and it is likely that the longer troops remain in Iraq and Afghanistan, the worse they will get.

Many soldiers' first instinctive response to witnessing the horrors of war is to repress their feelings and never talk about them. Traditional prescriptions for men to be tough intensify the expectation that, no matter how soldiers suffer, they should handle it alone. As more women take on combat roles, the same expectations now also apply to them. So, having seen a buddy blown to bits or realizing that they have killed an Iraqi child, many soldiers choose to suffer in silence. Some do so to protect their loved ones. Others fear the pain of telling their stories and not being understood.

That's what happened to one soldier serving in Iraq with whom I talked. He described how hard it was to sympathize with his fiancee in Dubuque when she wrote about daily frustrations like her car overheating, even as he was reeling from the shock of being reviled as an invader and occupier by the Iraqis around him. "It's hard to have any long-distance relationship," he told me, "but from Dubuque to the war in Iraq is impossible." After a three-week leave, he was headed back to the war zone, his engagement ended.

A Misguided Military Response

Help for traumatized troops must really begin on the battle-front. Yet the military's response has been largely inadequate, even misguided. When soldiers have breakdowns in combat, military therapists give them a little rest and a chance to talk with a counselor, then send them back into the fray, rationalizing that this helps prevent "survivor guilt." But sending psychologically fragile soldiers back into combat is wrongheaded; they'll likely feel guilt no matter what. Instead, therapists should advise commanding officers that these are the last people who should be sent back into battle. They should also seek ways to help the soldiers handle survivor guilt, such as pointing out that their deaths would not guarantee that others would live.

One military program, called Operational Stress Control and Readiness, or OSCAR, provides treatment in combat zones that includes antidepressant medication, usually Prozac. Though no one would begrudge a soldier anything that might dull the terror of combat, the truth is that the feelings they experience don't disappear and will have to be dealt with eventually. And there's something Brave-New-World-like about sending people into situations where they're endangered and feel helpless, and then when they crack, giving them drugs to change their brain chemistry so that they can return to battle.

The military also touts its debriefings for soldiers heading home. With these programs, which often last 10 days or fewer, it hopes to decrease the violent behavior some soldiers exhibit when they get back home. The Army increased its counseling after three soldiers back from fighting in Afghanistan were accused of killing their wives in 2002. Returnees are alerted that they may have nightmares and short tempers, reminded that their wives have been making all the decisions and may not want to give up that power, and warned that their young children might not recognize them. That's a good beginning, but for many, the debriefings are inadequate, and their very brevity can imply that this should be all they need to "get over it."

Devastating Realities

But even with forewarning, the reality of having your child fail to recognize you can be devastating. Some counseling may work for some soldiers, but other advice—buy some flowers for the wife, take the kids to Chuck E. Cheese—may fail to smooth the troubled waters of homecoming. It's no easy matter to know what will help, but even though the answers are neither simple nor obvious, the ongoing project of seeking them is a social responsibility.

Every one of us needs to shoulder a bit of the burden of helping our soldiers and our returning civilians with their re-entry into ordinary life back in the United States. In June [2004], I was at the bank when I heard a customer with red crew-cut hair boast, "We were with the 82nd that got Saddam." When the bank teller expressed awe, the soldier retreated a little, saying, "Well, I didn't actually see him. But some of our guys did." Another customer said, "Thanks for keeping us safe," and the soldier straightened up and boomed out that he was headed for Afghanistan soon. "Gonna get bin Laden," he declared loudly.

As he walked past me on his way out, I remarked quietly that I was frightened for him. His straight-as-a-board posture vanished, and he said, "I got stabbed in Iraq. We're sitting ducks. And it's weird being home. Can't stop watching my back." Given a chance to voice anything other than the expected bravado, out came his natural feelings of vulnerability. We need to let returnees say they were scared and let them know that's not crazy. We must also allow them to tell proud war stories when they want to. When they wish to talk, we must find non-psychiatric, non-pathologizing opportunities for them to do so openly, while also supporting them if they choose to see a therapist. And when they need silence, we must respect that, too.

Listening to Soldiers

In any case, a recent study in the *New England Journal of Medicine* revealed that enormous numbers of soldiers won't see therapists. It showed that 38 percent of soldiers thought to be mentally ill did not trust therapists, 50 percent worried that seeing one could harm their careers and a full 65 percent feared being seen as weak. Realistically, these barriers to therapy won't be overcome anytime soon.

So we citizens must accept the social responsibility of telling returnees not only that we will listen but that we will listen for as long as they want to talk about how it felt to be over there and how it feels to be back. We need to tell them not to censor themselves for fear of upsetting us, offending our sensibilities, making us feel helpless to help them or making us angry at them. If we fail to do this, then we become complicit in concealing some of war's most devastating consequences. And to refuse to face these fully is to increase the chances that we will go to war again.

| "*Mental disorders . . . prove strangely helpful to individuals who write, paint, sculpt and compose music.*"

Society Should Recognize Mental Illness as a Source of Creativity

Martin Gayford

The lives of great artists suggests that there is a link between mental illness and creativity, argues Martin Gayford in the following viewpoint. The painter Vincent van Gogh and the poet Lord Byron, for example, likely suffered from bipolar disorder, notes Gayford. Mental disorders such as depression and mania involve unusual thoughts and intense emotions that may spark the kind of creativity that produces great art, he explains. While having a mood disorder does not necessarily make one creative, many works of art hint at the influence of madness, Gayford concludes. Gayford writes for the Spectator, *a British magazine.*

As you read, consider the following questions:

1. How did the architect Francesco Borromini die, according to Gayford?

Martin Gayford, "Mad Genius," *The Spectator*, vol. 298, no. 9225, May 28, 2005, pp. 36–38. Copyright © 2005 by *The Spectator*. Reproduced by permission of *The Spectator*.

2. According to Arthur Koestler, cited by the author, what is creativity the result of?

3. What statistics suggest that mood disorders are more prevalent among artists?

In the summer of 1667 the architect Francesco Borromini—one of the most brilliant figures of the Italian baroque—fell into what was later described as a 'hypochondria,' complicated by fever. 'He twisted his mouth in a thousand horrid ways, rolled his eyes from time to time in a fearful manner, and sometimes would roar and tremble like an irate lion.' Doctors and priests were consulted, all of whom agreed that he should never be left alone, should be prevented from working, and all efforts made to encourage him to sleep so that 'his spirit might calm down'.

But these efforts were unavailing; the patient grew worse. The failure of his servants to obey his orders enraged him. On the night of 2 August he asked repeatedly for a light, a pen and some paper, but on doctor's orders was refused. Tossing in agitation, the great architect was heard to exclaim, 'When will you stop afflicting me, Oh dismal thoughts? When will my mind cease being agitated? When will all these woes leave me? . . . What am I doing in this cruel and execrable life?' He rose, found a sword—a standard piece of domestic equipment in that time and place—fell on it and pierced himself through the body from front to back.

However, he did not die immediately. Borromini lived for several hours, during which he saw his confessor and dictated an eminently lucid and detailed account of the extremely irrational process of thought by which he had come to kill himself. It describes how at around five or six in the morning he woke up and asked his servant Francesco to light a lamp, who replied, 'Signor, no.'

'And hearing this reply, I suddenly became impatient and began to wonder how I could do myself some bodily harm.'

Eventually, he remembered the weapon hanging at the head of the bed among consecrated candles, so he ran himself through. 'Because of the wound I began to scream, so Francesco ran in and opened the window, through which light was coming, and found me lying on the floor.' Only then, having described his own death, did Borromini die.

It is a terrible and gripping story, the narration of which was one of the high points of Anthony Blunt's lectures at the Courtauld Institute in the days before he was unmasked as a Soviet spy. There are distinct echoes in the botched and un-motivated suicide, the subsequent death-bed rationality, of the fate of Vincent van Gogh. But has it got anything more to tell us?

Art and Madness

It is hard to avoid describing Borromini's action as unhinged (though difficult to deny that his subsequent narrative is apparently sane). He was a man of eminently creative and original mind, and marked mental problems. It is noted that he fell into a deep melancholy because of the successes of his rival [Giovanni] Bernini. When a man was found damaging the fabric of his new work at St John Lateran in Rome, he ordered him to be beaten so severely that the vandal died—an action that suggests, in the terms of psychiatry, 'poor impulse control' and irritability (though architects to whom I have told this story invariably sympathise with Borromini's action).

The master was 68 at the time of his final crisis, and had designed some of the most original buildings not only of the 17th century but of all time. In his mind the language of Greek and Roman architecture became—so to speak—fluid and malleable like clay. He remodelled it in innumerable complex and beautiful ways. But was there a relation between his mental peculiarities and his imaginative achievements? For that matter, was there in the case of van Gogh? Is there, to put it bluntly and in old-fashioned terms, a link between madness and creativity? In various ways, some direct, some complex, perhaps there is.

A Classical Idea

This association is, of course, one of the most common in the history of the arts. Lord Byron, speaking of his fellow poets, remarked that, 'We of the craft are all crazy. Some are affected by gaiety, others by melancholy, but all more or less touched.' When he made that remark, the thought was already centuries old. . . .

[Poet John] Dryden put it most famously and succinctly, 'Great wits are sure to madness near allied/ And thin partitions do their bounds divide.' This link between madness and creativity was a venerable idea; indeed, properly speaking, a classical one: it goes back to Plato's belief that poets are inspired by 'divine fury' and Aristotle's observation that philosophers, poets and men outstanding in the arts tend to be 'melancholic'.

In the 19th century, the madness of poets and artists became a more fashionable belief, not only in the world of the arts. It was given serious consideration by the rising profession of psychiatry. The Frenchman Paul Möbius (1853–1907) studied what he called the *dégénérés supérieures*, a category that was accepted with enthusiasm by many artists and writers, who proudly considered themselves degenerate. . . .

Uncanny Creativity

Of course, there's a lot to be said for the view that great art is the opposite of mad. The music of Bach, for example, seems like the essence of calm, peace and emotional balance. Evidence suggests the great artists of the past in many cases—one thinks of Titian, [Peter Paul] Rubens and Raphael—were individuals of rude psychological health. I myself spend a great deal of time talking to artists, and find them—as a group—exceptionally intelligent and perceptive. To make art requires intense thought and determination as well as originality: as [critic Charles] Lamb put it, 'the admirable balance of all the faculties'.

None of that, however, means that making art—and creativity generally—does not exploit parts of the brain that are not used in routine affairs. There is clearly something mentally a little uncanny about artistic creativity. In his collection of essays *The Man Who Mistook His Wife for a Hat*, Oliver Sacks narrates the cases of Rebecca, a young woman with severe problems of thought and movement, and José, a teenage boy with autism brought on by childhood meningitis. Rebecca was unable to perform a task as simple as unlocking a door, and was clumsy and awkward in every movement—until she began to dance, at which point she became graceful. Mute for years, José turned out to communicate through drawing—at which he was astonishingly quick and accomplished.

Divine Fire

Arthur Koestler, in his study of this subject, *The Act of Creation*, proposed that all true creativity—not just artistic but also scientific and comic—resulted from a connection between two utterly disparate 'frames of reference'. This is likely to take place not as a result of conscious, rational thought, but to pop ready-made from the unconscious as a result of reverie, dream or just sleep. A celebrated example is the discovery by the chemist August Kekule (1829–96) that the structure of the benzene molecule is shaped like a ring.

The two disparate frames of reference which his unconscious brought together were chemical structures and reptiles. Wrestling with the benzene problem, the scientist sat down. 'I turned my chair to the fire and dozed. Again the atoms were gambolling before my eyes. . . . [My mental eye] could distinguish larger structures, of manifold conformation; long rows, sometimes more closely fitted together; all twining and twisting in snakelike motion. But look! What was that? One of the snakes had seized hold of its own tail, and the form whirled mockingly before my eyes. As if by a flash of lightning I awoke.'

This might be an example of what the Greeks meant by divine fire: inspiration coming as if from nowhere in a dream or a vision. Of course, a creative dream is not what we would call madness. However, there are also reasons to believe that mental disorders that cause misery, suffering and death can also prove strangely helpful to individuals who write, paint, sculpt and compose music.

Manic Depression

There is compelling evidence that many highly creative people both past and present suffered from manic depression—or, as it is now called by psychiatrists, bipolar affective disorder. Bipolar disorder may, in serious cases and for brief periods, cause symptoms that the man in the street would regard as deeply abnormal.

In extreme manic phases there may be hallucinations and delusions; Vincent van Gogh—whom I believe to have been manic depressive—experienced both at times, when he heard voices and saw sights that were not really there and thought wrongly that his neighbours were trying to poison him. But for the most part bipolar disorder does not cause such deep dementia; schizophrenia, which seems to have been much less common among artists and writers, does. It is a disturbance of the normal range of moods, causing deeper depression than an unafflicted person might experience, and greater highs of energy, wildly racing thoughts and euphoria. This condition recalls the mental state of Byron—a possible victim of bipolar disorder—as described by a friend.

His mind was 'like a volcano, full of fire and wealth, sometimes calm, often dazzling and playful, but ever threatening. It ran swift as the lightning from one subject to another, and occasionally burst forth in passionate throes of intellect, nearly allied to madness.' The composer Hugo Wolf, a bipolar case, spoke of how 'the blood becomes changed into streams of fire'. Virginia Woolf, in a moment of bravado, claimed that 'as

Fallen Artists

Despite depression's eclectic reach, it has been demonstrated with fair convincingness that artistic types (especially poets) are particularly vulnerable to the disorder—which, in its graver, clinical manifestation takes upward of twenty percent of its victims by way of suicide. Just a few of these fallen artists, all modern, make up a sad but scintillant roll call: Hart Crane, Vincent van Gogh, Virginia Woolf, Arshile Gorky, Cesare Pavese, Roman Gary, Vachel Lindsay, Sylvia Plath, Henry de Montherlant, Mark Rothko, John Berryman, Jack London, Ernest Hemingway, William Inge, Diane Arbus, Tadeusz Borowski, Paul Celan, Anne Sexton, Sergei Esenin, Vladimir Mayakovsky—the list goes on.

William Styron, Darkness Visible: A Memoir of Madness, *1990.*

an experience madness is terrific, I can assure you, and not to be sniffed at; and in its lava I still find most of the things I write about'.

This alternates with depression, characterised by bleak misery, lethargy, slowed thoughts and movements. It is a sort of seasonal change, and in fact seems often triggered by fluctuations in light levels. The 18th-century poet William Cowper compared his own depression to deep midwinter. 'The weather is an exact emblem of my mind in its present state. A thick fog envelops every thing, and at the same time it freezes intensely.' A great deal of art—much classical music, for example—is built round the alternation between these two opposites: the weeping and the laughter. In some cases—perhaps Van Gogh's—it is possible to get both phenomena at the same time: the mile-a-minute-mind plus intense depressive anxiety and panic.

Jamison's Research

In her book *Touched with Fire: Manic Depressive Illness and the Artistic Temperament* Kay Redfield Jamison, an American professor of psychiatry, makes out a powerful case that numerous great figures in the arts have been to one degree or another bipolar or unipolar (that is, depressive without manic phases). She deploys a great deal of evidence to show that this is the case.

Research she carried out in the late 1980s on a group of eminent British writers and visual artists produced striking results. One half of the poets in the sample had been treated in some way for mood disorders; nearly 20 per cent had either been hospitalised or required electroconvulsive treatment or lithium. Even more playwrights—63 per cent—were afflicted with depression, though had not received such drastic treatment. In comparison, biographers, novelists and visual artists showed much less dramatic signs of depression, but still well above the rates in the general population (bipolar is around 1 per cent, clinical depression around 5 per cent).

Another piece of her research, on British and Irish poets born in the 18th century, concluded that they were 20 times more likely to have been committed to a madhouse than their contemporaries, and five times more likely to have killed themselves. Somewhere between 60 per cent and 80 per cent of suicides are thought to be bipolar (which makes the very fact that Van Gogh, for example, shot himself an indication of what was the matter with him). Many more consider the step. 'I should,' Byron remarked, 'many a good day, have blown my brains out, but for the recollection that it would have given pleasure to my mother-in-law.'

These statistics, however striking, are inevitably vulnerable to the criticism that it all depends on which sample you choose. Dutch painters, for example—poor Vincent apart—seem a level-headed crowd. Even more convincing, I find, is that Jamison is able to put forward an explanation of how manic depression, and also straight depression, might actually aid creativity.

How Depression Aids Creativity

This could happen for several reasons. Firstly, there is the enhanced intensity of experience, both ecstatic and appallingly sorrowful, that these conditions bring. Jamison, who is herself bipolar, has described her own experiences in her book, *An Unquiet Mind*. 'The countless hypomanias [that is, mild manias], and mania itself, all have brought into my life a different level of sensing and feeling and thinking. Even when I have been most psychotic—delusional, hallucinating, frenzied—I have been aware of finding new corners in my mind and heart. Some of those corners were incredible and beautiful and took my breath away and made me feel as though I could die right then and the images would sustain me. Some of them were grotesque and ugly and I never wanted to know they were there or to see them again.'

Here, then, is one advantage provided by this kind of adversity. To an extent art is concerned with intense feeling, and the sufferers of these syndromes feel more—often unbearably more—than most of us.

Sanity is admirable in many ways; in comparison bipolar disorder is a terrible and quite often lethal affair. But sanity is more pleasant in part, it seems, because it is something of an anaesthetic against painful experience; or at least, it seems that the mildly depressed have a more realistic view of their lives than the non-depressed. This would help to explain the resistance that powerful art so often encounters. People do not like brutal facts, as the painter Francis Bacon observed, 'or what used to be called truth'.

The contrary-mood mania and the milder hypomania, with their enhanced energy and racing ideas, are conducive not only to feeling but also to original thinking. If Koestler was correct in believing that creativity comes from bringing together two apparently utterly dissimilar facets—thoughts, images, objects—then it is possible to see how the manic state might help. But Jamison makes the point that all this is experienced and suffered by people who for much of the time—perhaps all—are entirely balanced and lucid.

Of course, having a mood disorder doesn't make you creative. As philosophers say, it's neither necessary nor sufficient: you don't need it and just having it isn't nearly enough. But the more one considers the evidence, the more it seems that many great artists have experienced extreme emotional states in this way. . . .

Madness Combined with Sanity

So what does all this tell us about Borromini? According to Jamison's research, architects are, with biographers, among the artists least likely to experience mood disorders. This makes sense: architecture is a practical and, frequently, a conventional business. Most buildings follow a prevailing style.

But Borromini was a most unconventional architect, so much so that he became posthumously avant-garde. Successful during his lifetime, his work was denounced for centuries afterwards as being anarchic, capricious, fanciful, debauched, chimerical—in other words, too original for the age of reason. His impulsiveness, melancholia, irritability and suicide all fit the profile of bipolar disorder.

What made his buildings endlessly fascinating, however, was not just the novelty of their design, but the intellectual and mathematical rigour with which those ideas were developed. In the same way, what was amazing about his suicide was not that he did it, but how he described it. As Blunt put it, that 'combination of intense emotional power and rational detachment' are among the qualities that go to make him a great architect.

You might say something like that of all the poets, painters and musicians discussed here. It was not just having extreme emotional experiences and strange ideas that made them remarkable, it was also the ability to fit them into a new order. So, one might conclude, a kind of madness and absolute sanity combine in many a creative act.

| *"It turns out that the evidence linking depression to creativity is shaky."*

Society Should Not View Mental Illness as a Source of Creativity

Peter D. Kramer

In the following viewpoint Peter D. Kramer challenges the notion that mental illness, particularly depression, spawns creativity. As Kramer points out, depression has become romanticized because of the long-standing belief that it is a necessary element of the artistic temperament. But there is no consistent evidence proving this, he points out. In fact, studies have shown that the energy needed for creativity is often hampered by mood disorders. The public needs to recognize that depression is a serious illness that needs to be treated, not a source of inspiration that deserves protection. Kramer is a psychiatry professor at Brown University. He is also the author of Listening to Prozac *and* Against Depression.

As you read, consider the following questions:

1. What flaws does Kramer cite from early studies on creativity and depression?
2. How could depression and mania work to an author's benefit, according to the author?
3. What does the author say about suffering and art?

Perhaps the most common favorable belief about depression is that it inspires great creative efforts. Heroic melancholy may be dead, but the depressive artist is with us still, in imagination. That's why Prozac leads directly to [Vincent] van Gogh.

But it turns out that the evidence linking depression to creativity is shaky. And once we have found depression to be especially dangerous, we might demand quite solid evidence— might say that the bar has been raised, in terms of the proof that would satisfy us.

Part of the problem concerns melancholy, the empty sack. Early modern studies of madness and genius looked mostly at psychotic disorders, especially schizophrenia. More recently, the important work has focused on manic depression, also called bipolar affective disorder, and its variants. Most of the research that linked art and melancholy had only a tangential relationship to depression.

Mania and Creativity

Bipolar disorder is the illness that comprises various sequences of depressive and manic episodes. Manic depression has its own vast scientific literature; to do the topic justice would require another book. But if we are to discuss genius, there is no avoiding a quick orientation.

Mania is characterized by racing thoughts, frenetic activity, impulsivity, irritability, and poor judgment. Manics can be euphoric, but sometimes the state is painful—tears and intense anxiety can be signs of mania. In their manic phase, manic-depressives are often delusional, grandiose, and paranoid. Despite points of overlap, manic depression appears to be a distinct disease from major depression, differing in its genetics, gender distribution, pattern of medication response, and biological markers. To give one example: when manic depression affects the hippocampus, the abnormalities appear to be in a different type of neuron than the ones most affected in depression. In bipolar patients, the hippocampus can be *hyper* active, with cells firing more than usual, albeit in disorganized fashion.

In the literature on creativity, a good deal of attention is paid to hypomania, an agitated state—it can occur also as a personality trait—that sits just shy of mania. Hypomanics are expansive, energetic, and pleased with themselves. Recent studies of creativity emphasize the importance of confidence and positive mood, along with a moderate willingness to question conventional wisdom. One current image of the creative thinker—and also of the business executive, salesman, preacher, or publicist—is the hypomanic.

Early Studies

Bipolar affective disorder, the full-blown disease, may have ties to literary production as well. The most-quoted, best-designed modern study of creativity and mental illness is a pilot project, conducted in the 1970s and '80s and never replicated. Nancy Andreasen, an eminent psychiatric researcher, looked at thirty members of the faculty of the Iowa Writers' Workshop, the program where Philip Roth, Kurt Vonnegut, and John Cheever once taught. She compared the thirty teachers to thirty control subjects matched for age and social class. The writers had a marked excess of mood disorder (now using the phrase broadly), especially manic depression and alcoholism.

Andreasen's findings were strong—faculty members were bipolar or alcoholic in numbers that were unlikely to be due to chance alone. The small study was influential in turning attention to mania as a writerly trait.

More widely read than Andreasen's research, which it cites, is Kay Redfield Jamison's book length consideration of mood and creativity, *Touched with Fire*. The study is a labor of love, based on dozens of interviews conducted and hundreds of reference sources read. Jamison is herself bipolar; her book's bibliography alone would make a quiet argument for the benefits of a high level of energy. Jamison concludes that manic depression *is* the artistic temperament. Flights of fancy, mercurial moodiness, tempestuous brilliance, visionary imagination, brooding, morbidity, despair, sensuality, mutability—all are aspects of bipolarity. Jamison makes the claim most strongly for poets, notably British poets born in the eighteenth century. [William] Blake, [William] Wordsworth, [Samuel Taylor] Coleridge, [Lord] Byron, [Percy Bysshe] Shelley, and [John] Keats are in the group. In effect, Jamison's book considers the narrow version of heroic melancholy—that it leads to lyric verse—and centers the relevant pathology in bipolar affective disorder, not major depression.

In speaking with scientists about research on depression, I have also asked their opinion of the state of our knowledge about mood disorder and creativity. The responses have been reasonably uniform, that there is not enough good data on the heroic melancholy hypothesis in any of its versions—but that, as regards mania and poetry especially, there may well be something there.

Problems With Research

The experts mention a number of technical problems. Biographical material may not yield precise diagnoses. (Do we count van Gogh as manic, or epileptic? How do we factor in [Edgar Allan] Poe's alcoholism and epileptic symptoms?) Because artistic success depends on prevailing tastes, inclusion criteria become dicey; if a study looks at poets whose work is gathered in standard collections, the sequence of events that led to the choice of poems and authors comes into play. Do anthologists value depressive poems, or rely on the judgment of generations that did? It turns out to be hard to get outside the culture, influenced as it has been by centuries of fascination with heroic melancholy.

If the association between bipolarity and creativity is real, how it works remains unclear. Does manic depression constitute an original perspective? Is the disease associated with genes that produce compensatory talents? Or is it a matter of energy only? Or of inflated self-esteem? Because it includes vigor and confidence, hypomania, which can persist for long intervals in manic-depressive patients, seems helpful in any number of careers.

Jamison's research suggests as much. She finds connections between bipolarity and leadership in science, business, religion, politics, and military affairs. That is to say, she has also revived the broad theory of heroic melancholy, again centering it on bipolar affective disorder, not major depression.

If manic depression confers a benefit, it may be through increased productivity in general. Never mind the aching heart and drowsy numbness, if you are not reasonably busy and self-assured, you can't die young of tuberculosis, as Keats did, and leave a body of poems behind. Perhaps for a romantic poet, the combination is ideal—enough depression to create familiarity with the morbid themes that literary convention values, and then the manic flight that gets the work done. In contrast, the dense and steady depression of patients like Betty and Margaret and Mariana [case studies of depressed individuals] lacks compensatory "fire," the vigor and decisiveness and electrifying leaps of mind that characterize a certain sort of creative fertility.

In this field, psychobiography, the shift of interest away from unipolar depression has been especially striking. Recent research into the writing patterns of Emily Dickinson, once a standard example of the depressive poet, has revealed periods of intense production suggestive of bipolarity. In terms of presumptive diagnosis, an extraordinary number of writers and artists have moved in recent years from depressed or schizophrenic to bipolar. Jamison counts Edgar Allan Poe, Ezra Pound, and Virginia Woolf in this category. Regarding her own work, Jamison once told me, "I write when I'm manic and edit when I'm depressed," not a bad formula for an author.

Depression vs. Mania

Given this recentering of heroic and poetic melancholy, you might expect to find an extensive philosophical literature that debates the ethics of treating or preventing bipolar affective disorder or mania. There is not nearly the volume of writing that addresses depression. But then, even before evidence emerged, as it has recently, that bipolar disorder is associated with brain anomalies, we had come to accept that bipolarity constitutes pathology. Manic depression appears to be highly heritable. Manic episodes cause disruption out of proportion to any psychological cause. Mania ruins families quickly and brutally, through destructive acts that include suicide, violence, and the spending down of fortunes. Mania seems unnatural. To interrupt agitation is to restore normality.

Or perhaps it is that the metaphorical tradition is missing, mania as depth. It is true that the frenzy of Greek heroes for the most part sounds manic. Ajax slaughtered flocks of livestock—his colleagues' spoils of war—thinking they were his enemies; then he turned his sword on himself. But the romance of melancholy—[Johann Wolfgang von] Goethe, Keats, [Thomas] Carlyle—revolves around despair. Manic depression may produce poetry; it may even produce poetic souls whose life stories move us—think of Anne Sexton or Robert Lowell. But taken by itself, mania is likely to remind us of getting and spending. Hypomania is the affliction our society demands and induces. It is the disposition of traders and salesmen. The evidence of creative productivity notwithstanding, connotatively, mania is inauthenticity and surface.

I have often thought that this difference in connotation contributes to the contrast in our perceptions of medications for the different diseases. Lithium and the other mood-stabilizing drugs used in manic depression can be dangerous, in their secondary effects. And in principle, medicines that flatten mania—again, lithium is the best studied—should be suspect, as regards the squelching of creativity. In practice, bipolar patients often do complain that they are less imaginative on lithium. In one study of bipolar artists stabilized on lithium, a quarter said that the medication interfered with their creativity. (Half said it helped, because "lithium prevented their barren depressions and their overactive manias resulting in artistically valueless works.") But metaphorically, lithium prevents frenetic action and induces the serene, contemplative state valued by the ancient Greeks. And so there are few news stories about the side effects of antimanic compounds.

As depression achieves full status as a disease, apprehensions about treating it effectively should wane, as they have in the case of bipolar affective disorder. In any event, the objective evidence associating creativity with depression is weak. In the Andreasen study, depression appears twice as often in the Iowa writers as in the control group. But (as is not true for bipolarity) the numbers are too small to make the comparison meaningful. Also, there is just so much alcoholism in the sample—far more than among depressives in general—that it is hard to tell what role depression plays. Did alcoholic depressives invite one another into the academic department, creating a society tolerant of drinking? As for Jamison, she refers to depression, but for the most part, her research findings and her passion concern bipolarity. When we go back and look at studies we imagined made the link between creativity and depression, often we find that they deal with other diseases that were once grouped with depression in the catchall, melancholy.

Mood Disorder and Creativity

Because objective evidence is lacking, we are left to consult our experience about the relationship between mood disorder and creativity. Certainly on a day-to-day basis, depression looks like a straightforward handicap. Patients tend to report that they did more and better work before they were depressed; and they do more and better work once they recover.

It is true that *difference* helps in the creative process, and depression is a form of difference. And of course, creative people make use of what life hands them. Some of the writers I have known, as friends and as patients, are odd enough. But the oddness is hardly all of one type.

A few writers have a minor variant of autism; they are awkward socially, and their conversation resembles lecture more than dialogue. Some writers struggle with a chronic sense of derealization; experience is distant from them, in a fashion that resembles the sensibility of certain epileptics, between seizures. Other writers live almost too insistently in the instant, the bon vivants and raconteurs. They are sprightly and funny, all glittering surface, in the manner of manics or even smooth-talking sociopaths. There are paranoid writers. Narcissism comes with the territory. Depression, yes—patients who are depressed and creative tend to seek me out, as a writer-doctor with an interest in mood disorder. But depression is one condition among many. Writing thrives on particularity, originality, distinctive voice and standpoint.

Mania, epilepsy, alcohol abuse—if we were to reconstruct the notion of the disturbed genius, we would need to replenish melancholy quite thoroughly. Don't some writers make their way via obsessionality, poring over the same patterns repeatedly? Although we may not be convinced that writers need to be eccentric; writers can be ordinary, to the extent that anyone is.

When I think of the relationship between depression and writing in particular, I prefer to imagine a complex process of mutual adaptation, between the disease and the medium. Think of the moment when the voyage of adventure becomes internal. Perhaps there are many such moments—in John Bunyan, Shakespeare, Carlyle. Long before James Joyce reworks the *Odyssey* into interior monologue, the contemplative man styles himself the picaro, encountering demons and exploring strange territory without leaving his study.

If accounts of innerness constitute art, then the natural storytellers are those who have journeyed farthest and lived to tell the tale. Mania and depression are the antipodes. And perhaps depression has special standing. It is frightening, disorienting, and alarming, entailing as it does loss of faith in self. If self-consciousness is the subject of art, depressives are the ideal chroniclers.

Which is fortunate, since writing has long been held forth as a treatment for depression. If isolation begets melancholy, still, writing, so Renaissance authors say, is a specific against despair. Besides (in our time), writing is something that the depressed can do. Mustering the stamina for a regular job may be difficult, and conforming to the set hours, and composing the "game face" necessary to make a sale or inspire a team. Social intercourse may be painful. But paper is patient. It is available in the small hours, when insomnia rules. Writing can be set aside and then resumed. Words are subject to revision. Depressives, it is said, have little energy, but that little they apply doggedly. Perhaps this trait relates to the scrupulosity that German researchers note. It does not take much time to produce art, if one is good at it. Graham Greene set himself a goal and limit of 500 words a day. He would stop in midsentence. Afternoons were spent indulging his ennui. Think how

101

prolific Greene was. Later in life, he cut back to 300 words. Writing may have the same appeal for depressives that it has for stutterers, another well-represented group.

As for greatness, it seems a vexed concept. It has been some years since we have imagined, in nineteenth-century fashion, that the spirit of the times shows through in a single creative soul. Who is our great artist, after Picasso? What writers are replacing [John] Updike, [Saul] Bellow, and [Philip] Roth? Did those men fill the shoes of [James] Joyce, Woolf, and [William] Faulkner, never mind [Charles] Dickens and [Leo] Tolstoy? Today, each of us is free to compose his own list, without reference to a canonical notion of the towering figure or to a universal image of the zeitgeist.

If we were comfortable with greatness, would depression, the illness, be a requirement? Our lack of conviction, regarding the linkage of art and depression, is evidenced by our long reach backward, to the nineteenth century, for examples. I have never been asked, "How will the availability of Prozac affect John Updike's work?"

"Not much" would be the answer—I mean, according to our imaginations. I have no way of knowing whether Updike has taken antidepressants. But our notion of melancholy no longer extends to embrace a man like Updike, a writer who seems, on the face of it, playful and affable, entranced by the pleasures and ironies of daily living.

I mention Updike in the spirit of memoir. Along with Saul Bellow, he represented contemporary art, the part of it I aspired to join, throughout my formative years. I particularly loved an early Updike short story, "The Alligators," about a fifth-grade boy who dreams of rescuing a new girl in the class, who is being teased by others. He reaches out to her, but too late: "It came to him that what he had taken for cruelty had been love, that far from hating her everybody had loved her from the beginning, and that even the stupidest knew it weeks before he did. That she was the queen of the class and might as well not exist, for all the good he would get out of it." The overtone of [Søren] Kierkegaard in Updike's story, the wonderful confusion of altruism and selfishness, sympathy and self-pity, was right up my alley. The plot speaks to the injuries of daily life, humiliations universally endured—but without need of reference to depression.

Updike is the fictional diarist of a generation, the recorder of a time and place, postwar America. His predominance throughout the second half of the twentieth century reminds us of the appeal of art grounded neither in sadness nor in profound and determined alienation. In Updike, limitations of character take their toll, terrible events ensue, conventional perspectives prove shaky, until there is no fixed point to stand on—and yet, wonder at the world's riches is never absent. Even catastrophe is redeemed by faith and humor. Updike is one of many writers whose work suggests that heroic melancholy is more a matter of literary convention than medical reality.

Updike writes in the tradition without being of it. I am thinking particularly of his early work *The Centaur*. It was the novel assigned my freshman class the summer before our arrival at college—my first glimpse of what the university understood as literature. The book plays off the myth of Chiron, the centaur of the book's title. Chiron was the teacher of heroes: Jason, Achilles, and Hercules. Because he suffered from a never-healing wound, inflicted by one of Hercules' arrows, Chiron ceded his immortality to Prometheus, bringer of fire, who was then himself condemned to eternal pain. Both Chiron and Prometheus are icons of creativity.

Updike frames a contemporary novel around the classic myth. His Chiron is George Caldwell, a burnt-out schoolteacher struck in the foot by a student's arrow. An equally resonant wound is borne by George's fifteen-year-old son Peter, the Prometheus figure, who worries over the social consequences of his psoriasis. Work, aging, chance, and the inevitable failures of courage or of judgment—these suffice to wear away at a man. Grace, love, and sexual possibility provide compensations. The movement of the book is toward Peter's maturation, toward his awareness of the joys and burdens of creation. *The Centaur* is Updike's [James Joyce's] *Portrait of the Artist*. We understand that Updike's will be the art of the socially aware and socially integrated, art that can find inspiration in the modest victories of daily life.

Psoriasis, Updike later revealed in an autobiographical essay, is his own affliction. (He wrote of his stuttering, too, and his asthma; do we imagine that more is better?) On occasion, Updike will impose psoriasis on a fictional character, as an ongoing humiliating loss. "The name of the disease, spiritually speaking, is Humiliation," one Updike character concludes. He is a potter, and as his skin improves, the quality of his pots, and of his love life, declines. But wonder at nature's handiwork is never absent in Updike. In *The Centaur*, Peter Caldwell confesses: "The delight of feeling a large flake yield and part from the body under the insistence of a fingernail must be experienced to be forgiven."

Skin eruptions may once have constituted melancholy, but no longer. They do allow, in Updike's fiction, for adherence to narrative convention. We have the form of heroic melancholy, but with key elements muted. The template can stand on its own, shaping a story that involves neither mental abnormality nor (in the contemporary, human characters) grand genius.

Melancholy in Fiction

There is, perhaps, room for embarrassment in confessing a devotion to Updike's work. By recent critical standards, he is precisely not melancholic enough; had Updike (so the rap on him goes) personally suffered more, his work might be deeper and he would evince broader sympathies. Cynthia Ozick complains that Updike's "fictive world is poor in the sorrows of history." Sorrow is the operative word. Political events and scientific discoveries serve as framework and metaphor in Updike's major novels. His writing is steeped in history. But the use is mutedly optimistic and American (consider the moon landing, as background in *Rabbit Redux*), rather than thoroughly bleak and European.

Not so the domain of that other hero of my youth, Saul Bellow. His best-known protagonist, Moses Herzog, inhabits the nightmare of history. He travels to Poland, is shaken by thoughts of the Holocaust. Most famously, he corresponds, in mind and on paper, with writers and philosophers long dead. His affinities are well placed: "[George] Hegel understood the essence of human life to be derived from history. History, memory—that is what makes us human, that and our knowledge of death."

Though Herzog is in his forties, his fictional memoir adopts the arc of the youthful novel of self-formation. A romantic failure leads to despair, then the temptations of alienation, and finally a more or (as in Herzog's case we suspect) less stable happiness rooted in acceptance of cultural norms.

Herzog announces his disorder in the first sentence: "If I'm out of my mind, it's all right with me." His quest is mostly internal and spiritual, but it has pronounced physical, geographic movement as well. He makes mad dashes from the Berkshires toward Martha's Vineyard, then to Manhattan and Chicago, and back to the Berkshires. Herzog is the frenzied melancholic, self-centered, self-righteous, voluble, irritable, impulsive, and enraged. As readers, we accept the convention; we accord Herzog his brilliance and (tattered) nobility. Traits on the manic spectrum serve well as indicators of heroism.

In James Atlas's recent biography of Bellow, the novelist appears to have a good deal in common with his protagonist. Bellow is self-absorbed, given to self-pity when abandoned, and occasionally hypochondriacal. He is energetic, seductive, vain, vengeful, and mistrusting. And he is a genius. Bellow is a melancholic malcontent, where that category stands apart from depression.

Depression not a Prerequisite for Creativity

Because art comments on what has come before, because stories rely on and play off readers' expectations, because depression and recovery from depression inform our notion of the story line, heroic melancholy persists in art—even in the work of writers who are not themselves depressed. Perhaps the pairing will continue indefinitely; perhaps it will fade in the face of improvements in treatment. With the advent of antibiotics, infectious disease waned in importance as a source of plot and emotion. There was no second *Bohème*, no second *Magic Mountain*, until the era of *Rent* and *Angels in America*, responses to a new untreatable contagion, HIV-AIDS.

But then, depression is grander than tuberculosis, in its cultural effects. To write seriously is to comment on *Hamlet* and *Don Quixote*. Once a tradition is established, it draws the energies of writers of all stripes—a truth of which *Hamlet* and *Quixote* may themselves be examples.

I don't imagine that Shakespeare was depressed, nor [Miguel de] Cervantes, for all that their great protagonists are melancholics. Cervantes was a military hero who lost the use of his left arm in one of the glorious battles of his era. Late in life, he imagined a reader addressing him as "the cripple who is sound, the great man, the jolly writer, and, in short, the joy of the Muses!" No one knows what Shakespeare and Cervantes were like. But we are free to imagine them vigorous, hearty, productive—resilient.

For the present, not only depressives, but all writers will want on occasion to don the mask of the wounded aesthete or the frenzied malcontent, as a narrator or protagonist. But in life, if suffering enriches art, it seems that any form will do: stuttering, asthma, hypochondriasis. No one would propose preserving bipolarity or alcoholism or epilepsy in order to maintain a supply of anguished artists of the sort Kierkegaard honored. Depression has a lesser claim, when it comes to creativity. Depression may relate to creativity only in the fashion of quite plebeian diseases and handicaps, like psoriasis or the narcissist's fragile ego.

Periodical Bibliography

The following articles have been selected to supplement the diverse views presented in this chapter.

Monica Anzaldi and Maureen Buell — "Building Collaboration Between Criminal Justice and Mental Health," *Behavioral Health Management*, July/August 2005.

Dennis Behreandt — "Psychiatry and the State," *New American*, November 15, 2004.

Jennifer Gonnerman — "Where Justice and Mercy Meet," *Village Voice*, July 28–August 3, 2004.

Melissa Healy — "Depression's Machismo Mask," *Los Angeles Times*, October 17, 2005.

Ron Honberg and Darcy Gruttadaro — "Flawed Mental Health Policies and the Tragedy of Criminalization," *Corrections Today*, February 2005.

Julia Lutsky — "Mentally Ill Abandoned by the System," *People's Weekly World*, November 6, 2003.

Diana Mahoney — "Addressing Depression in the Workplace," *Clinical Psychiatry News*, March 2005.

Mary Beth Pfeiffer — "Changing of the Guards," *Legal Affairs*, July/August 2005.

Ralph Slovenko — "The Trouble with Szasz," *Liberty*, August 2002.

Cynthia Stankiewicz — "The ADA and Psychiatric Disabilities," *Ability*, January/February 2005.

Thomas Szasz — "Civil Liberties and Civil Commitment," *Freeman*, December 2003.

Jane Tanner — "Mental Illness Medication Debate," *CQ Researcher*, February 6, 2004.

CHAPTER 3

What Mental Health Issues Do Youths Face?

Chapter Preface

The statistics on teen suicide are disturbing. In the United States suicide is the third leading cause of death for fifteen- to-nineteen-year-olds. Each year, about 20 percent of all high school students consider committing suicide, and nearly 10 percent attempt it. Because the majority of suicidal youths are suffering from depression, parents, counselors, and psychiatrists are focusing more attention on recognizing symptoms of the disorder and on finding effective antidepressant therapies for children.

Several studies have shown that low levels of serotonin, a mood-regulating hormone, can cause depression. Antidepressant drugs know as selective serotonin reuptake inhibitors (SSRIs) work by slowing down the reabsorption of serotonin into the neural system, thereby increasing the serotonin level in the brain. Over the past two decades, tens of millions of people have combated depression with the help of such SSRIs as Prozac, Paxil, and Zoloft, among others. Currently, about 5 percent of American fifteen- to-eighteen-year-olds are prescribed SSRIs—a 50 percent increase over teens who were prescribed these drugs in 1998.

More recent studies and insights about the adolescent brain, however, have made doctors wary about prescribing antidepressants for youths. Several studies concluded that a small but significant percentage of young people who take SSRIs become suicidal, particularly in the first few days and weeks of use. Since antidepressants lift the feelings of fatigue and lethargy associated with the disorder before they counteract feelings of despair, they may energize and agitate a depressed teen enough so that he or she acts on suicidal thoughts. In addition, the brains of adolescents differ in many ways from adult brains. The prefrontal cortex—the region of the brain responsible for controlling impulses and inhibiting dangerous thoughts—is not fully functional until the early twenties.

Thus, young people are more prone to act on their impulses, including self-destructive ones, than adults are, scientists say. For this reason, the energizing and disinhibiting effects of antidepressants pose more of a threat to youths than to adults, researchers point out.

As a result of these discoveries, in October 2004 the Food and Drug Administration (FDA) directed manufacturers of antidepressants to include a "black box" warning on their product labels. This label alerts health care providers to an increased risk of suicidal thoughts and behavior in young people being treated with these drugs. Currently, Prozac is the only medication approved by the FDA to treat depression in children, and psychiatrists and parents are cautioned to observe young patients closely for any signs of adverse reactions to the drug.

Some health officials are concerned that parents and physicians are overreacting to the "black box" label, however. The number of antidepressant prescriptions for youths under eighteen dropped 10 percent in 2004. But many researchers point out that antidepressants still benefit the majority of depressed children. For example, the suicide rate among teens has dropped as the use of SSRIs has increased: The rate for fifteen- to twenty-four-year-old males fell from twenty-three per one hundred thousand in 1994 to seventeen per one hundred thousand in 2000. In 2006 the overall teen suicide rate was eight per one hundred thousand. David Fassler of the American Psychiatric Association maintains that SSRIs should not be abandoned: "I do worry that some parents may be frightened and confused by the numerous media reports and may be reluctant to seek help for their children with psychiatric disorders. There are very significant risks of not treating an illness like depression."

These concerns about adolescent depression are further explored in the following chapter, which also examines the debates surrounding autism and mental health screenings for youths.

| "No one knows what causes autism or why more children are developing it."

Childhood Autism Is a Serious Problem

Shari Roan

Autism, a neurological disorder that can cause profound difficulties in communicating and interacting with people, is on the rise among children, reports Shari Roan in the following viewpoint. Experts are discovering ways to diagnose autism at earlier ages, which is of great benefit because early interventions and therapies can greatly improve an autistic child's functioning. Doctors and health-care insurers often deny early diagnostic tests, however, because they are expensive. Thus, parents who suspect that their child may be autistic find it difficult to obtain the help that they need. Roan is a staff writer for the Los Angeles Times.

As you read, consider the following questions:

1. By what percentage did California autism cases increase between 1987 and 1998, according to Roan?
2. What behaviors are associated with autism in children, according to the author?

Shari Roan, "For the Autistic Child, Time Matters," *Los Angeles Times*, February 14, 2005, p. F1. Reproduced by permission.

3. What kinds of problems have parents encountered after their child received a very early diagnosis of autism?

Dr. Pauline Filipek sizes up her tiny patient in her toy-strewn clinic in Orange [California]. As the 22-month-old boy enters the room, he doesn't look at Filipek or anyone else. He plows into a pile of toys on the floor, sometimes walking or crawling over them, but doesn't speak.

He could easily pass as a good-natured child who needs little attention. But Filipek, a neurologist, sees something else, behaviors "that make the hair on the back of my neck stand up." Most toddlers will carry a toy in only one hand—this child clutched a toy in each fist when entering the room. And children this age typically will scope out a room full of strangers warily, sticking close to Mom or Dad for reassurance.

The scene is familiar to Filipek. At the end of a 90-minute exam she tells the child's parents that their son has autism. Filipek pulls her chair close to the couple, first-time parents in their 30s, and leans toward them before she continues. "The fact that you're here with him, this young, is *wonderful*."

It is balm intended to soothe the harsh news. And Filipek's encouragement is sincere. She is among a growing number of child development experts who say that autism often can be identified much younger than is typically done today, and that early treatment can alter, sometimes dramatically, the course of the brain disease that affects about one in 500 U.S. children.

Geraldine Dawson, director of the Autism Center at the University of Washington's Center on Human Development and Disability, says doctors now can reliably diagnose autism by age 2 and researchers are developing screening tools to identify kids as young as 18 months. "The long-range goal," she says, "is to be able to detect autism at birth or in very early infancy."

Cases on the Rise

Early recognition is one of the most hopeful developments in the sobering world of autism, a neurological disorder in which people have difficulty communicating and interacting socially with others. Autistic children often speak little, ignore others and display repetitive behavior, such as spinning in circles or focusing on one object for hours. They may excel at something in detail, such as spelling or playing a musical instrument, but become overwhelmed when trying to navigate the world at large. The disorder is also known as "autism spectrum disorder," reflecting the wide range in severity of cases and the various subtypes of autism, such as Asperger's disorder and pervasive developmental disorder.

In California, an estimated one in 322 children has been diagnosed with autism, according to the state Department of Development Services (DDS). According to its 2002 report, autism cases increased 273% from 1987 to 1998. Between 600 and 800 children with autism are added to the DDS's service rolls every three months. No one knows what causes autism or why more children are developing it.

Many doctors see the effort to diagnose autism earlier as a significant development that could yield clues to what causes autism and how best to treat it.

The Diagnostic Dilemma

But the trend in early diagnosis has also created a backlog of parents who are demanding diagnostic evaluations earlier—often for babies. Doctors and insurers frequently deny these services for several reasons: Evaluations are costly, there is a lack of trained therapists and some healthcare providers say that autism can't reliably be identified before age 3 or 4.

"It's like there are two camps. You have some doctors—the few—who are comfortable diagnosing children at the age of 1," says Rebecca Landa, director of the Center for Autism and Related Disorders at the Kennedy Krieger Institute in Baltimore. "And you have others who feel strongly that you can't diagnose before age 3. They won't even talk about it. Research on early diagnosis is coming off the press as we speak; it's that recent. People are just starting to list what the red flags are in infants and toddlers."

Those lists are beginning to make their way into the hands of parents and pediatricians.... A lack of nonverbal communication could be one of the first signs that a child isn't developing normally, experts say.

Signs of Autism

At about 8 months, Dawson says, babies should babble and pay attention when their names are called. By 12 to 14 months, they should point, wave, gesture, imitate others and play peekaboo.

"This is the age when the child points at something and looks at the mother to see if she sees it," she says. "They show things to their parents. Even before kids are using formal words, they are using their bodies for pointing and showing. This is important because with a child with autism both the verbal and nonverbal systems are affected."

Although these behaviors are subtle, they are proving to be fairly reliable diagnostic tools. In a 1994 study, Dawson and colleagues examined videotapes of the birthday parties of year-old children later diagnosed as autistic and compared them with videos of normal children. Researchers watched for four behaviors: looking at others, gesturing and pointing, showing things, and responding when their names were called. They weren't told which children were later diagnosed as autistic. Nevertheless, they were able to correctly identify 10 out of 11 normal children and 10 out of 11 autistic children.

Other potential signs of the disorder can emerge between the first and second birthdays, experts say. While most toddlers will be speaking at least a few words by 14 to 18 months, autistic children often do not. Delayed language development may not by itself indicate that a child is autistic, but a delay combined with other autism symptoms is reason for concern, doctors say.

Also, an estimated 20% of children with autism appear to develop normal speech, but then begin to regress, no longer speaking words they once spoke, growing silent, shunning others, becoming isolated.

Doctors can only identify symptoms that may indicate autism in very young children, says Filipek, noting that the earlier the diagnosis is made, the greater the chance of misdiagnosing a child. Still many experts say they feel it's better to recognize any developmental delay and address it as early as possible, no matter what the disability is labeled.

Acting on Instinct

While doctors look for specific developmental signposts, many parents are relying on their own awareness of rising autism rates and a "gut feeling" to bring their children in for evaluations at younger ages than ever before.

Cindy Bluth had read about autism in women's magazines and knew enough about the disorder to begin worrying when her daughter, Juliette, was 7 months old. Cindy had three older children when she married her husband, Jon, in 2000.

"I know a little bit about babies," says Bluth, picking up scattered toys in the family room of her San Clemente home one recent morning. "I realized that Juliette never really looked at Jon and that my face should be her favorite 'toy,' but she did not want to look at me." Juliette was also not babbling.

When her daughter was 10 months old, Bluth called the pediatrician—telling herself she was being silly. "You don't want to be this parent who thinks everything is wrong all the time." But the pediatrician agreed that Juliette's silence and avoidance of eye contact was unusual and said he wanted to see the baby again in two months. By then, Juliette was walk-

Behaviors to Watch For

Possible symptoms at 6 months:

- Not making eye contact with parents during interaction

- Not cooing or babbling

- Not smiling when parents smile

- Not participating in vocal turn-taking (baby makes a sound, adult makes a sound, and so forth)

- Not responding to peekaboo game

At 14 months:

- No attempts to speak

- Not pointing, waving or grasping

- No response when name is called

- Indifference to others

- Repetitive body motions such as rocking or hand flapping

- Fixation on a single object

- Oversensitivity to textures, smells, sounds

- Strong resistance to change in routine

- Any loss of language

At 24 months:

- Does not initiate two-word phrases (that is, just echoes words)

- Any loss of words or developmental skill

Rebecca Landa, Center for Autism and Related Disorders at the Kennedy Krieger Institute, Baltimore

ing on her toes (a characteristic of autism) and spent hours engrossed in the same Disney videotape.

For Bluth, the clincher came one day when she sat in the park and watched as Juliette sifted through gravel for 40 minutes, engrossed. "I decided then I wasn't going to sleep another night without finding out what was wrong," she says.

Juliette was diagnosed with autism at UC [University of California] San Diego shortly after her first birthday.

Urging Parental Vigilance

In her clinic near UC Irvine Medical Center, Filipek says most early diagnoses result from parents' concerns, not pediatricians' referrals. In one 1997 study of 1,300 families, children were diagnosed with autism, on average, at age 6. However, many of the parents had sensed something was wrong when their children were about 18 months old, and they had sought medical assistance, on average, by age 2.

"Parents say, 'I have known something is wrong since they were 12 months old, and I've been from physician to physician to physician and they always say not to worry,'" Filipek says. "If you think something isn't right, 85% of the time you are on the money as a parent."

The [Centers for Disease Control and Prevention's 2005] campaign aims to educate pediatricians about symptoms while urging parents to reject "wait and see" advice from a doctor.

"I think doctors are afraid of misdiagnosing this," says Bluth, who credits her pediatrician for listening to her early concerns. "The benefits of starting therapy early are so great. How is it going to hurt them to be evaluated? A misdiagnosis wouldn't be the end of the world."

An Intervention Backlog

The controversy over early diagnosis can create obstacles after a child has been identified as autistic. Brodie and Karen Sadahiro's daughter, Grace, 3, was diagnosed with autism by

UCLA physicians at 26 months. Despite a 14-page diagnostic report from UCLA, doctors at a local treatment clinic—which contracts with the state to provide free or low-cost services—rejected the family's request for therapy, saying autism cannot be diagnosed before age 3.

After filing two lawsuits and threatening a third, the Sadahiros obtained an autism diagnosis and services for Grace late [in 2004]. "Most of us do not have enough money to fund our own therapy," Karen Sadahiro says. "So we have to wait until after age 3. What is the point of early diagnosis if you can't get early intervention?"

Many autism treatment centers are set up to deliver therapy to preschool and older kids only, Landa says. While more doctors are making early diagnoses, she says, "the centers aren't prepared for it. The money isn't there."

Although there is little research to support its usefulness, most autism experts say that intensive therapy—which usually includes 20 or more hours a week of behavioral, speech, physical and occupational therapies—can improve a child's functioning. The earlier such therapy begins, the better, they say. Kids with autism must be taught what comes naturally to other children.

"We don't know yet whether early intervention will give us more of an advantage," says Filipek. "But autism is like a deprivation experience. We feel that if we can stimulate, very early in life, those areas of the brain that are emerging and developing, we can change the course of development."

New Discoveries

Early, aggressive interventions have already disproved some notions about the disorder, says Catherine Lord, director of the University of Michigan Autism & Communication Disorders Center.

For example, doctors used to believe that about half of all autistic people couldn't talk. But in Lord's sample of children diagnosed at age 2 and undergoing therapy, only 14% were still nonverbal by age 9 and about 35% to 45% could speak fluently.

Lord contends that many children who are diagnosed young and receive three to four years of intensive therapy can enter regular elementary schools and function independently. Her long-term study following children diagnosed at 2 found that about 5% no longer have autistic symptoms at age 9, while an additional 20% have some symptoms but can attend regular schools. The remainder improve but continue to have difficulties.

Children who undergo intensive therapy can sometimes progress so well that they appear normal by preschool age and are denied further services. The responsibility for providing therapy to developmentally delayed children typically switches from regional centers to public school districts at age 3.

Kai's Story

Diagnosed as autistic shortly after his first birthday, Kai Viruleg underwent extensive therapy and was able to converse, look at strangers and enter preschool by his third birthday. But because he no longer exhibited autistic behaviors, the school district denied Kai access to several of his previous therapies. His mother, Jennifer Damian, had to fight to restore his services, hiring a lawyer at one point. Meanwhile, some of Kai's autistic behavior reemerged.

"It has taken me about three months to line up new services, and he has lost a lot of ground," says Damian, of Northridge [California]. "Regression comes very quickly. It only takes a week of missed therapies."

Damian's determination—she quit her job to become his full-time advocate—has given Kai a chance he may not have had. Most days, Damian shuttles her son to therapy appointments, doctors' visits and school from 8 a.m. to 8 p.m. After almost two years of intense intervention he is on track to enter a normal elementary school.

"I remember the day he was diagnosed, after I finished bawling I said, 'I'm going to cure him of his autism,'" Damian recalls. "Well, autism is not a curable disorder. But he would have been severely autistic at this point if we had done nothing."

> "*Studies of highly intelligent children show them to have many of the characteristics that ... are an open invitation to false diagnoses of autism.*"

Many Diagnoses of Autism Are False

Thomas Sowell

Diagnoses of childhood autism are often false, argues syndicated columnist Thomas Sowell in the following viewpoint. So-called experts can be too quick to label certain common childhood behaviors, such as a preference for solitude or starting to talk at a later age, as symptoms of autism, he points out. The notion of an "autism spectrum" aggravates this problem of mistaken diagnoses, Sowell contends, because the spectrum includes too wide of a range of behaviors. The reports of a recent increase in autism may be due to the redefinition of autism rather than a higher incidence of the disorder, he writes.

As you read, consider the following questions:

1. What comparison does Sowell use to expose what he believes is a problem with the idea of an "autism spectrum?"

Thomas Sowell, "The Autism 'Spectrum,'" *Conservative Chronicle*, September 17, 2003, p. 29. Copyright 2003 Creators Syndicate. Reproduced by permission of Thomas Sowell and Creators Syndicate, Inc.

2. What kinds of children are often wrongly diagnosed as autistic, according to the author?

3. According to Sowell, why are some parents urged to allow their children to be labeled autistic?

When Billy's mother sees her 12-year-old son's popularity with teammates on his baseball team, she thinks back to predictions made when he was a pre-schooler that he would have so much trouble making friends that, among other things, he would probably never be able to get married and have children.

It is a little early for Billy to be getting married, but the predictions have been off by miles so far. Why were such dire predictions made in the first place?

Billy was late in beginning to talk and was supposed to have been autistic. Once that label had been put on him, nothing could change the minds of those who saw him that way.

Contrary evidence from his emotional attachment to a little girl in his pre-school was dismissed, even though the two of them were inseparable on the playground—and even though an inability to form emotional attachments is at the heart of autism.

Redefining "Autism"

There is another kind of dogmatism from people who are not going to give up on the "autism" label. That is redefining the word to include a wide range of children who are said to be on the autism "spectrum." Billy's mother raised a fundamental question that seems to have eluded many professionals: Would you say that someone who is near-sighted is on the "blindness spectrum"?

What would we gain by such manipulations of words? And what would we lose?

Blindness, like autism, is a major tragedy. When some little toddler doesn't see quite as well as other kids, and may need

A Debate on Autism

What lies behind the increase in cases is sharply debated. To some, the upswing has all the hallmarks of an epidemic and indicates that autism itself is increasing rapidly.

To others, the rise can in large part be explained by increased public awareness of autism in recent years, changes in the way the disorder is diagnosed and the incentive of tapping into federally mandated services for autistic children. . . .

[Epidemiologists] point to flaws in the way that the rising numbers—especially those in California—have been presented to the public. And they say the small size and widely varying findings of epidemiological studies of autism make it impossible to say what is going on.

For example, Dr. Eric Fombonne, an epidemiologist and a professor of child and adolescent psychiatry at McGill University, said most of the increase was probably a result of diagnostic changes and statistical anomalies.

Erica Goode, New York Times, *January 26, 2004.*

glasses, what would be the point of alarming his parents by saying that he is on the blindness spectrum?

In the decade that has passed since I organized a support group of parents of late-talking children in September 1993, I have heard from literally hundreds of parents of such children, many of them re-living the anguish they went through when their children were diagnosed as autistic.

With the passage of time, it has become obvious that many of these children are not autistic, any more than Billy is autistic. Parents who are grateful that the hasty diagnoses their children received were wrong are also bitter that such labels were applied so irresponsibly—often by people who never set foot in a medical school or received any comparable training that would qualify them to diagnose autism. But professionals have been wrong as well.

Wiggle Room

Instead of trying to reduce mistaken diagnoses that inflict needless trauma on parents and often direct children into programs for autistic children that are counterproductive for children who are not autistic, the expansive new concept of an "autism spectrum" provides wiggle room for those who were wrong, so that they can avoid having to admit that they were wrong—and avoid having to stop being wrong.

It is as if people who told you that your little toddler would need a seeing-eye dog are able to get off the hook when the passage of time proved them wrong by saying that, because he now wears glasses, he is still on the blindness spectrum.

The Irresponsibility Spectrum

There is another aspect of this that affects the public in general and the taxpayers in particular. Time and again over the past decade, parents have told me that they have been urged to allow their late-talking children to be labeled "autistic" so that they would be eligible to get government money that can be used for speech therapy or whatever else the child might need.

Against that background, consider the widely publicized statistics showing an unbelievable rate of increase in autism in recent years. Is this a real change in the same thing or a redefinition of words? Worse yet, is this the corrupting effect of government money intended for children who are genuinely autistic?

Apparently no one knows the answer. But what is very disturbing is that such questions are not even on the agenda.

Studies of highly intelligent children show them to have many of the characteristics that can get them labeled autistic if they happen to be late in beginning to speak. For example, the book *Gifted Children* by Ellen Winner shows that such children "often play alone and enjoy solitude," have "almost obsessive interests" and "prodigious memories."

Such characteristics are an open invitation to false diagnoses of autism by those who are on the irresponsibility spectrum.

| "Modern antidepressants ... are credited with the small but real decline in overall [teen] suicides seen in the past few years."

Depressed Teens
Need Antidepressants

Part I: Bernadine P. Healy; Part II: Betsy Bates

According to the authors of the following two-part viewpoint, teen depression is a crisis that demands more attention. In Part I, former National Institutes of Health director Bernadine P. Healy maintains that teen suicide is often the result of depression, a mental disorder that can be especially devastating for adolescents. In Part II, Betsy Bates, a reporter for Clinical Psychiatry News, *explains that parents are understandably concerned about studies that have concluded that certain antidepressants can increase the danger of suicide among youths; however, untreated depression is far more dangerous. A combination of cognitive behavioral therapy and antidepressant medicines remains the best strategy for combating teen depression, Bates reports.*

As you read, consider the following questions:

1. What part of the brain is responsible for the emotional mood swings that teens experience, according to Healy?
2. How often does an adolescent commit suicide in the United States, according to Bates?
3. What is the median age of onset for depression, as stated by Bates?

Part I

His death brought forth white ribbons. White, not black, because that's the color of grief when young innocents depart this world. [In November 2003], this seemingly happy jokester, computer whiz, and talented high school sophomore took his own life. His death tore through the hearts of his fellow students, parents, and teachers at my daughter's close-knit school, all wondering what had spiraled out of control in his young mind and what might have been done to save him.

The same questions arose with the news of three recent student suicides at New York University. What despair would throw them to their violent deaths? The fact is that suicide is in all our neighborhoods, in all our schools, in many of our families, unpredictably taking some 30,000 people a year. That's similar to the number who die each year from breast or prostate cancer and twice the number from AIDS. But when it comes to those 4,000 to 5,000 suicides among the tender young—10 to 24 years old, the age of self-imagined immortality—we are looking at a disease that carries a special chill.

Minds in Tumult

Teens look healthy, even adult, yet their minds are in tumult. We've long known that the human brain undergoes extensive shaping and pruning in the first few years of life. But recently we've discovered that another remodeling spurt occurs around puberty and extends into the 20s. For teens, the "gut response" part of the lower brain, the amygdala, rules. This tiny bundle of nerves mediates emotions like fear, anger, and anxiety. As teens mature, their frontal lobes, the domain of reason and judgment, increasingly rein in the amygdala, and the notorious emotional swings of teen life level out.

Just when amygdaloid behavior moves into the danger zone is not always clear. Be it nature or nurture, for some more sensitive souls, seemingly ordinary stresses of school or social life—academic disappointments, embarrassments, and romantic break-ups—can trigger crushing emotional pain and suicidal despondency. To be sure, teens suffer more than they let us know and more than we tend to remember. Brain-imaging studies now tell us that emotional hurt stirs the brain at precisely the same sites that physical pain does. And the more intense the hurt, the more of a spike in neuronal activity. One can only imagine the agony of suicidal teens and young adults, wanting yet unable to reach out and desperate for relief.

A Lethal Form of Despair

Indeed, most of these young people are dying of a lethal form of despair. In both depression and suicide, levels of serotonin, the brain's mood hormone, are abnormally low. Modern antidepressants that boost it are credited with the small but real decline in overall suicides seen in the past few years. But [in 2003] the Food and Drug Administration cautioned that some of these drugs when used in those under 18 might increase suicidal behavior. This again highlights how little we know about what's really going on in churning teenage minds. More important, it leaves us in a quandary, particularly for doctors treating the several million young people who survive suicide attempts each year.

Boys at Risk

A universal and perplexing reality is suicide's maleness. Our boys kill themselves six times more often than do girls. In

2000, the United States had 4,294 recorded suicides among the 10-to-24-year age group; only 632 of them were girls. This despite the fact that females are diagnosed with depression more often and make many more suicide attempts. A closer look suggests that males often experience and express their illness differently—more aggression, anger, irritability, and impulsiveness and less of the overt hopelessness, helplessness, and sadness common in suicidal females. Boys just don't use girls' vocabulary or body language when they're emotionally hurting.

Young suicide inspires no March of Dimes, Race for the Cure, or colored lapel ribbons. Let's face it, it's a disease that hits too raw a nerve. Yet this silent epidemic cries out for attention. We need better data on just what is and isn't normal in the background noise of teenage life and on how to get through the wall of prickly emotions with the right therapies. We must ask ourselves why emotional, social, and spiritual wholeness so often plays second fiddle to academic prowess. And we must focus on our sons, who bear the greatest brunt of this mortal disease. We will never catch our young before they fall unless every parent—indeed, every one of us—feels their pain.

Part II

Some antidepressant medications may increase suicidal ideation in pediatric patients, but untreated depression is deadly without question, David Feinberg, M.D., said at a meeting sponsored by the Los Angeles Pediatric Society.

"The thing that doesn't get said on CNN [Cable News Network] is that this disorder kills people," stressed Dr. Feinberg, medical director of neuropsychiatric and behavior health sciences at the University of California, Los Angeles.

He outlined the magnitude of the problem: 9% of adolescents report attempting suicide; suicide now accounts for 12.5 deaths/100,000 adolescents, up from 5/100,000 in 1960; and an adolescent commits suicide every 90 minutes in the United States.

Warning Signs of Depression and Suicidal Feelings

Self-destructive behavior and involvement in dangerous activities are signs that a teen may have little or no regard for his or her personal safety or life. Many suicidal teens will live life on the edge by driving fast, playing dangerous games with weapons, or playing chicken with their cars and bikes. Any sort of high-risk activity of this type merits attention.

Promiscuous sexual behavior is often an attempt to sedate strong feelings of failure and depression. Kids who see themselves as worthless, unloved and rejected will look for acceptance and love through sexual intimacy.

Drug and alcohol abuse is another factor contributing to suicide. While their abuse appears to contribute to suicide by aggravating or exaggerating depressed feelings and suicidal tendencies, their use can also point to the presence of depression and suicidal feelings.

Walt Mueller, youthculture@today, June 2005, www.cpyu.org/.

Dr. Feinberg acknowledged that the effectiveness of antidepressant medications in adolescents is far less clear than it is in adults, who have a much lower placebo response. Among 40 studies in adolescents, just 2 have clearly demonstrated effectiveness, largely because placebo response rates are in the range of 60%.

Yet the median age of onset of depression is 19. It is the third leading cause of death among 15-to 19-year-olds, and the fourth leading cause of death among 10- to 14-year-olds.

Treating Depression

Just how to treat it has become more of a conundrum than ever before, with the Food and Drug Administration's decision [in 2004] to impose a black box warning on all antidepressant drugs regarding an increased risk of "suicidality" in pediatric patients.

In addition. Dr. Feinberg explained that a review of studies showed a 1% incidence of new onset suicidal ideation among pediatric patients assigned to placebo and a 2.7% increase in suicidal ideation among those patients who are receiving antidepressants.

Some drugs, including venlafaxine (Effexor) and escitalopram (Lexapro), were more strongly associated with suicidal ideation risk than others, he said, but not one study subject actually committed suicide among the 4,400 enrolled in antidepressant trials.

Regardless of whether the black box warning is received among physicians, parents are bound to be more leery than ever of antidepressants for their children. Primary care physicians, in particular, are spooked as well.

Various Therapies Are Necessary

Dr. Feinberg's advice, plainly stated, is to stick with research proven results.

"Every [depressed pediatric] patient should be in cognitive-behavioral therapy," he suggested, describing the technique as a practical, concrete reframing of thoughts that is highly effective in children and adolescents.

However, not all pediatric patients respond quickly or robustly to cognitive-behavioral therapy (CBT) alone.

"If the depression is moderate to severe, you're going to get into trouble by not giving an antidepressant," Dr. Feinberg warned.

His advice in the absence of new research is to stick to the only antidepressants with proven efficacy in pediatric patients: fluoxetine, which is available in a generic formulation; or sertraline (Zoloft) if the child has comorbid obsessive-compulsive disorder.

Dr. Feinberg strongly cautioned physicians about the lack of evidence to support prescribing multiple psychotropic medications in depressed children.

"There literally are no data," he said. "Less is better. There is no evidence that multiple medications are more effective and the interactions can be horrendous."

Knowing the Risks

In light of new fears, he recommended that all depressed pediatric patients should be seen frequently: at least on a weekly basis, not monthly, at the onset of antidepressant therapy and whenever doses are being increased.

Families must be thoroughly educated about the risks inherent in untreated depression and the risk of increased suicidal ideation because of medication.

Patients must be counseled to share any new thoughts about suicide, and the threshold for calling the doctor should be set very low.

Any suicidal patient should be hospitalized and treated with antidepressant medication in conjunction with CBT, he stressed.

Because CBT may play an increasingly pivotal role in the treatment of pediatric depression, many audience members asked Dr. Feinberg how he selects referral sources.

The specific degree of a counselor (psychologist vs. licensed clinical social worker) is less important than solid training in cognitive-bahavioral therapy, he said. The fact that a counselor is on the patient's preferred provider list is low on the priority list, he said.

> *"Antidepressants can create what's called an 'activation syndrome' in depressed children—giving them the energy to act on suicidal thoughts."*

Antidepressants Can Be Dangerous for Teens

Susan Schindehette

The same medicines commonly used to combat depression lead to an increased risk of suicide in some youths, writes Susan Schindehette in the following viewpoint. Schindehette recounts the story of Julie Woodward, a depressed teen who committed suicide only one week after she began taking the antidepressant Zoloft. Some adolescents experience agitation when they first begin taking antidepressants, which can then compel them to act on suicidal thoughts. Parents and physicians need to become more informed of the risks associated with antidepressants and the symptoms that signal potential suicide attempts, the author concludes. Schindehette is a senior writer for People *magazine.*

As you read, consider the following questions:

1. According to Schindehette, what symptoms are danger signals for patients who have just started taking antidepressants?

2. How many children in the United States take antidepressants, according to the author?

3. What signs indicated that Julie Woodward might have been having an adverse reaction to Zoloft, according to Schindehette?

From the very beginning, Tom and Kathy Woodward's first-born was a golden child. At 5 months, she spoke her first word. While still in preschool, she was signed by the Wilhelmina agency as a child model. And by the time Julie Woodward reached her sophomore year at a Catholic high school near her home in North Wales, Pa., she was a good student looking forward to a bright future that would include, as she once wrote on a piece of paper titled "Plan for Life," marriage (anytime "over 26"), children ("two or three") and "a nice house in the country."

Instead, at 16, Julie's life took a dark turn. In the fall of 2002 she began having trouble at a new school and, in defiance of her parents' wishes, began dating a college boy. Julie became quiet and withdrawn, so much so that in July [2003, her parents] Tom and Kathy took her to a psychiatrist, who prescribed two antidepressants. She lasted on the medication just one week: On July 23, after discovering that their daughter wasn't home—and hadn't spent the night with her grandparents, as they had thought—her parents became alarmed. Tom walked out to the garage behind the house, opened the door and found Julie, 17, dead. "She had hanged herself," he says, his voice breaking. "I grabbed her, and I knew she was gone. I felt her, and she was cold."

A Growing Concern

Today, eight months after the tragedy, the Woodwards still sound as if they are trying to convince themselves that all of this really happened. "Julie was the most self-protective, self-preserving kid in the world," says her mother, Kathy, 47. Adds

Tom, 46, who, like his wife, is a financial consultant: "I never in a million years thought this could happen to us."

But it did, and the Woodwards aren't the only parents to suffer such a loss. On March 22 [2004] the FDA [Food and Drug Administration] issued a recommendation for manufacturers to begin printing warning labels for antidepressants, in response to growing concern that the very drugs meant to lift kids out of depression sometimes do just the opposite. "The labeling we are proposing won't say you can't use these drugs," says Dr. Thomas Laughren of the FDA psychiatric drugs division. "[But] the one thing that was clear from our hearings is that many patients were not being well monitored." The labels will caution patients to watch for signs of hostility and agitation, especially during the first days of use and whenever dosage is adjusted.

Exact figures on the number of children on antidepressants who have killed themselves are impossible to come by. In February [2004], 31 families—including the Woodwards—traveled to Washington, D.C., to testify before an FDA panel. There, anguished parents told of sons and daughters who became agitated, aggressive and, in the most extreme cases, suicidal, sometimes within days of the drugs' being prescribed. In addition to warning labels, the agency has ordered further scrutiny of the drugs, many of them SSRIs (for selective serotonin reuptake inhibitors), which, in rare circumstances, have also been suspected as a factor in adult suicide. "We want to make sure if there is the slightest indication these drugs cause suicide that children not be exposed to that," says U.S. Rep. Jim Greenwood (R-Pa.), who has called on drug companies to release unpublished research on the subject. "Right now we are trying to fit the pieces together and sort this thing out."

Youths and Antidepressants

It may come as a surprise to parents just how little testing has been done on kids and antidepressants to date. About 1 mil-

The Dangers of Akathisia

In some people, SSRIs [selective serotonin reuptake inhibitors] induce a sensation called *akathisia*, a restless agitation that ranges from mere jitteriness to feeling you're "jumping out of your skin."

Researchers have been aware that SSRIs could trigger *akathisia* at least since 1990, when Harvard investigators reported on a group of six adult patients taking Prozac for depression who developed "intense violent suicidal preoccupation" after taking Prozac for two to seven weeks. Their fixation with violence and death abated when they stopped taking the drug. Similar symptoms were noted the next year in a paper describing six children aged 10 to 17 who developed "intense self-injurious ideation or behavior" on Prozac. One 14-year-old girl, who'd been depressed but never suicidal, began cutting herself and chanting that she wanted to die after three weeks on the drug.

Rob Waters, Psychotherapy Networker, *January/February 2004.*

lion children are now taking the drugs, sold under names like Prozac, Celexa and Paxil, and the majority report side effects no more serious than dry mouth and sleeplessness. The benefits, meanwhile, when used in conjunction with other therapy, can be huge. Paradise Valley, Ariz., mother Sherri Walton, 45, describes antidepressants as a lifeline for her 15-year-old daughter Jordan, who has battled Tourette's syndrome, depression and obsessive-compulsive disorder. "Now I have a happy, healthy teenage child who's successful in school and can't wait to get her learner's permit," says Walton. "Her medication helped every step of the way."

Yet some doctors complain that information is scarce when it comes to kids and antidepressants. In all, just 4,000 children have taken part in clinical trials for antidepressants. Only one of the drugs, Prozac, carries official FDA approval for treating kids with depression. (Because of the complex way medicines are introduced to the market, other antidepressants that have proven safe and effective in adults may be legally prescribed "off-label.") "[At this point], we're not sure how children and adults react differently," says Dr. Philip Walson, director of clinical trials and pharmacology at Cincinnati Children's Hospital Medical Center. "We need to test these drugs and monitor them and realize that children aren't just little adults." For its part, Pfizer, the company that manufactures Zoloft, declines to comment specifically on the Woodward case, although a vice president, Dr. Catherine Clary, says that it will work closely with the FDA to devise label changes for the drug.

Julie's Story

Caution comes too late for the Woodwards, whose three-story stone house in the Philadelphia suburbs is the kind built for a large family. "You live for your children," says Tom, who coaches track while Kathy teaches Sunday school. Julie, an older sister to Caroline, 16, and brothers Tom, 12, and Brian, 8, was always precocious and introspective. "She was more the observer," says Kathy. As a toddler, "she wanted to go to the park and just see the other kids. She didn't want to be part of the crowd."

But Julie was no loner. At Gwynedd Mercy Academy, her private high school, she played sports and sang in the choir. "Her friends here would say she was a very creative person, a good writer and a good friend," says the school's principal, Sister Kathleen Boyce. But for her junior year, Woodward decided to transfer to a much larger public school. "She wanted the real high school experience," says Kathy. The transition was tough. Julie's grades suffered, and she abandoned old friends and activities. She also began secretly dating the 19-year-old brother of one of her friends. The relationship ended, but not before Julie had stayed out all night and been involved in a minor car accident the next day. "Julie was very depressed," says Lindsay Harris, 17, who had known her since fourth grade. "If you talked about school, she didn't want to talk about it. If you talked about the future, she didn't want to talk about it."

Kathy Woodward was the first to bring up the idea of counseling for her daughter. "I drove her to the doctor, but she wouldn't get out of the car," says Kathy. The Woodwards eventually had Julie examined by two doctors before a third diagnosed her with depression. Julie enrolled in a group-therapy program at the Horsham Clinic in Ambler, Pa., where the admitting doctor prescribed Zoloft and trazodone, the generic name for another antidepressant often used on patients who are having trouble sleeping. Kathy says she was initially opposed to medicating Julie but, told it was an important part of her therapy, deferred to mental health professionals.

Julie took her first Zoloft [on] July 16 [2003], and, six days later, after complaining of insomnia, began taking trazodone. Her moods were mixed: Some days she seemed sweet and contented. On another she argued with Kathy and shoved her to the floor. "I got up and hugged her and said, 'What's that?'" recalls Kathy. "She just kind of looked surprised. It took a few seconds, but she hugged me back."

"The Whole Thing Was Shocking"

In the days that followed, Julie celebrated her younger brother's birthday with the family and helped pack for vacation. On the night she died, Kathy left the house to take her three younger kids to softball and a swim meet. Tom was already driving home from work at the time. Out of the blue, Julie called him from home and said that Kathy wanted him to come directly to the swim meet. "I told her I loved her," says Tom, barely able to collect himself. "She told me she loved me too."

The Woodwards weren't terribly concerned that Julie wasn't at home when they returned that night, since she routinely spent nights at her grandparents' house nearby. But the next day, a counselor from the Horsham clinic called to say Julie had missed a therapy session. Now worried, Kathy said she wasn't sure exactly where her daughter was, to which the therapist replied, "You have to find her. Julie had a terrible session on Monday," recalls Kathy. It was later that day that Tom found Julie's body in the garage.

In the wake of her death, police confiscated the teen's computer and journals, and found no mention of suicide. But the family did discover what Tom describes as a "goodbye note" in a backpack that Julie had left at her grandparents' house days earlier. "The whole thing was shocking," says her friend Jacqueline Cellucci, 17. After a period of depression, Julie "seemed much happier. I thought she was fine."

Activation Syndrome

In retrospect, the Woodwards say there may have been signs that Julie was having an adverse reaction to the drug. Her sister Caroline, who shared a room with Julie, now says that Julie, lying in bed, said she was experiencing the feeling of being lifted up toward the ceiling. Other family members recall seeing Julie pacing back and forth in her bedroom several days before the suicide, and rocking back and forth—both possible signs of a condition called akathisia, which can include agitation. (Akathisia has been reported as one of Zoloft's adverse reactions.) An autopsy determined that Julie had a higher-than-expected level of the antidepressant in her blood, which may indicate she was not absorbing the drug as quickly as other patients.

As in other cases of adolescent suicide, impulsivity may have also been a factor. According to Dr. Norman Fost, a University of Wisconsin pediatrician and bioethicist, antidepressants can create what's called an "activation syndrome" in depressed children—giving them the energy to act on suicidal thoughts. "I don't think these drugs should be prohibited," says Fost, "but anyone prescribing them to adolescents needs to tell parents about the risks."

That is now the Woodwards' fervent hope. Since Julie's death, they've torn down the old wooden garage where she ended her life. But there are other things they cannot bring themselves to do—closing out her checking account or choosing a headstone for her grave, which they often visit. Grappling with questions that may always remain unanswered, they insist there's at least one thing they're certain of. "If it hadn't been for that drug," says her father, "Julie would still be here with us."

"Our Nation [must] adopt a comprehensive, systematic approach to improving the mental health status of
children."

Government-Sponsored Mental Health Screenings Would Benefit Children

President's New Freedom Commission on Mental Health

*President George W. Bush established the President's New Free-
dom Commission on Mental Health in April 2002 to identify future government policies that would benefit adults and children
with mental disorders. In the following excerpt from the
commission's 2003 final report, the twenty-two commissioners
outline strategies to promote children's health and prevent childhood mental disorders from worsening. Emphasizing the importance of early detection and early treatment of mental illness, the
commission recommends that all public school children undergo
mental health screenings. Federally funded school health programs should also provide care and treatment for mentally ill
children, the commission argues.*

President's New Freedom Commission on Mental Health, "Achieving the Promise:
Transforming Mental Health in America," www.mentalhealthcommission.gov.

As you read, consider the following questions:

1. What percentage of students with serious emotional disturbances drop out of school, according to the author?
2. What is meant by the phrase "co-occurring disorder," as used by the commission?
3. What specific suggestions does the commission make for strengthening mental health programs in schools?

For consumers of all ages, early detection, assessment, and linkage with treatment and supports can prevent mental health problems from compounding and poor life outcomes from accumulating. Early intervention can have a significant impact on the lives of children and adults who experience mental health problems.

Emerging research indicates that intervening early can interrupt the negative course of some mental illnesses and may, in some cases, lessen long-term disability. New understanding of the brain indicates that early identification and intervention can sharply improve outcomes and that longer periods of abnormal thoughts and behavior have cumulative effects and can limit capacity for recovery.

Untreated Disorders Can Lead to a Downward Spiral

Early childhood is a critical period for the onset of emotional and behavioral impairments. In 1997, the latest data available, nearly 120,000 preschoolers under the age of six—or 1 out of 200—received mental health services. Each year, young children are expelled from preschools and childcare facilities for severely disruptive behaviors and emotional disorders.

Since children develop rapidly, delivering mental health services and supports early and swiftly is necessary to avoid permanent consequences and to ensure that children are ready for school. Emerging neuroscience highlights the ability of environmental factors to shape brain development and related behavior. Consequently, early detection, assessment, and links with treatment and supports can prevent mental health problems from worsening.

Without intervention, child and adolescent disorders frequently continue into adulthood. For example, research shows that when children with co-existing depression and conduct disorders become adults, they tend to use more health care services and have higher health care costs than other adults. If the system does not appropriately screen and treat them early, these childhood disorders may persist and lead to a downward spiral of school failure, poor employment opportunities, and poverty in adulthood. No other illnesses damage so many children so seriously. . . .

Schools Can Help Address Mental Health Problems

Currently, no agency or system is clearly responsible or accountable for young people with serious emotional disturbances. They are invariably involved with more than one specialized service system, including mental health, special education, child welfare, juvenile justice, substance abuse, and health.

The mission of public schools is to educate all students. However, children with serious emotional disturbances have the highest rates of school failure. Fifty percent of these students drop out of high school, compared to 30% of all students with disabilities. Schools are where children spend most of each day. While schools are primarily concerned with education, mental health is essential to learning as well as to social and emotional development. Because of this important interplay between emotional health and school success, schools must be partners in the mental health care of our children.

Schools are in a key position to identify mental health problems early and to provide a link to appropriate services. Every day more than 52 million students attend over 114,000 schools in the U.S. When combined with the six million adults working at those schools, almost one-fifth of the population passes through the nation's schools on any given weekday. Clearly, strong school mental health programs can attend to the health and behavioral concerns of students, reduce unnecessary pain and suffering, and help ensure academic achievement.

Co-occurring Disorders

Early intervention and appropriate treatment can also reduce pain and suffering for children and adults who have or who are at risk for co-occurring mental and addictive disorders. Seven to ten million people in the United States have at least one mental disorder in addition to an alcohol or drug abuse disorder. Too often, these individuals are treated for only one of the two disorders—if they are treated at all.

In his speech announcing the Commission, the President used an example that affirms this point. The President spoke of:

> ". . . a 14-year-old boy who started experimenting with drugs to ease his severe depression. This former honor student became a drug addict. He dropped out of school, was incarcerated six times in 16 years. Only two years ago, when he was 30 years old, did the doctors finally diagnose his condition as bipolar disorder, and he began a successful program. . . ."

Co-occurring substance use and mental disorders can occur at any age. Research suggests that as many as half of the adults who have a diagnosable mental disorder will also have a substance use disorder at some point during their lifetime.

A substantial number of children and adolescents also have co-occurring mental illnesses and substance use disorders. If one co-occurring disorder remains untreated, both usually get worse. Additional complications often arise, including the risk for other medical problems, unemployment, homelessness, incarceration, suicide, and separation from families and friends. . . .

Obstacles to Treatment

Studies show that few providers or systems that treat mental illnesses or substance use disorders adequately address the problem of co-occurring disorders. Only 19% of people who have co-occurring serious mental illnesses and substance dependence disorders are treated for both disorders; 29% are not treated for either problem. For people with less serious mental illnesses and substance dependence problems, the pattern of under-treatment is even worse. Most (71%) receive no treatment; only 4% receive treatment for both disorders. The same pattern of under-treatment holds for youth with co-occurring disorders. . . .

Of all the children they see, primary care physicians identify about 19% with behavioral and emotional problems. While these providers frequently refer children for mental health treatment, significant barriers exist to referral, including lack of available specialists, insurance restrictions, appointment delays, and stigma. In one study, 59% of youth who were referred to specialty mental health care never made it to the specialist. . . .

The Importance of Early Detection

Early detection and treatment of mental disorders can result in a substantially shorter and less disabling course of illness. As the mental health field becomes increasingly able to identify the early antecedents of mental illnesses at any age, interventions must be implemented, provided in multiple settings, and connected to treatment and supports.

Early interventions . . . and educational efforts can help a greater number of parents, the public, and providers learn about the importance of the first years of a child's life and how to establish a foundation for healthy social and emotional development.

Quality screening and early intervention should occur in readily accessible, low-stigma settings, such as primary health

Recommendations of the President's Commission

The time has long passed for yet another piecemeal approach to mental health reform. Instead, the Commission recommends a fundamental transformation of the Nation's approach to mental health care. This transformation must ensure that mental health services and supports actively facilitate recovery, and build resilience to face life's challenges. Too often, today's system simply manages symptoms and accepts long-term disability. Building on the principles of the New Freedom Initiative, the recommendations we propose can improve the lives of millions of our fellow citizens now living with mental illnesses. The benefits will be felt across America in families, communities, schools, and workplaces.

Michael F. Hogan, Chairman,
President's New Freedom Commission on Mental Health,
July 22, 2003.

care facilities and schools, and in settings where a high level of risk for mental health problems exists, such as juvenile justice and child welfare. . . .

A National Approach

The Commission suggests a national focus on the mental health needs of young children and their families that includes screening, assessment, early intervention, treatment, training, and financing services. The national focus will:

- Build on coordination mechanisms already in place, such as Part C of the Individuals with Disabilities Education Act (IDEA); and

- Expand the coordination of services for children ages 3 through 21 for those who qualify for services under Part B of IDEA, thus building capacity for improved and increased services in communities.

A coordinated, national approach to these issues will help eliminate social and emotional barriers to learning and will promote success in school and in other community settings for young children. This effort may involve collaborations among parents, mental health providers, and early childhood and child care programs. Other important dimensions of the approach will include:

- Training a workforce skilled in treating young children and their families;

- Training primary health providers to screen for and recognize early signs of emotional and behavioral problems and to offer connections to appropriate interventions;

- Eliminating barriers to coverage, such as a required psychiatric diagnosis when an alternative diagnosis that minimizes labeling and stigma is more appropriate; and

- Including "social and emotional check-ups" in primary health care.

The IDEA specifically provides for a statewide, comprehensive, interagency system for early prevention services for children with disabilities from birth to 3 years old who have a developmental delay and physical, cognitive, communication, social, or emotional or adaptive development problem, or have a diagnosed physical or mental condition that has a high probability of resulting in a developmental delay.

More effort is needed to heighten public awareness of the developmental requirements for children's social and emotional well-being—just as public awareness of the early developmental and educational needs for reading skills has been increased through public and private initiatives.

When children with disabilities reach age 3, they may be eligible for services under Part B of IDEA if they have one of the specified impairments and if, because of the impairment, they need special education and related services. However, services and other resources for children who have emotional and mental health issues are sometimes less readily available with respect to workforce, interventions, and financing, than other services, such as speech and language therapy or physical therapy.

Addressing the mental health of young children may also involve providing information, supports, and treatment for parents. For the young child, treating the parents' mental health problems also benefits the child.

School Mental Health Programs

Growing evidence shows that school mental health programs improve educational outcomes by decreasing absences, decreasing discipline referrals, and improving test scores. The key to improving academic achievement is to identify mental health problems early and, when needed, provide appropriate services or links to services. The extent, severity, and far-reaching consequences make it imperative that our nation adopt a comprehensive, systematic approach to improving the mental health status of children.

Clearly, school mental health programs must provide any screening or treatment services with full attention to the confidentiality and privacy of children and families. The Columbia University TeenScreen® program provides a model for early intervention.

The Commission recommends that Federal, State, and local child-serving agencies fully recognize and address the mental health needs of youth in the education system. They can work collaboratively with families to develop, evaluate, and disseminate effective approaches for providing mental health services and supports to youth in schools along a critical continuum of care. This continuum includes education and training, prevention, early identification, early intervention, and treatment. . . .

Removing Barriers to Success

The No Child Left Behind Act of 2001 is designed to help all children, including those with serious emotional disturbances, reach their optimal potential and achievement. To fulfill the promise of this Act, schools must work to remove the emotional, behavioral, and academic barriers that interfere with student success in school. Consequently, it is critical to strengthen mental health programs in schools. This effort may involve:

- Working with parents, local providers, and local agencies to support screening, assessment, and early intervention;

- Ensuring that mental health services are part of school health centers;

- Ensuring that these services are federally funded as health, mental health, and education programs;

- Building on a recommendation from the President's Commission on Excellence in Special Education to implement empirically supported prevention and early intervention approaches at the school district, local school, classroom, and individual student levels; and

- Creating a state-level structure for school-based mental health services to provide consistent State-level leadership and collaboration between education, general health, and mental health systems.

Since the IDEA requires that a variety of professionals collaborate in the school and in the community, the Commission urges that coordinating services be regarded as a "related service" in the child's Individual Education Plan (IEP). In developing the IEP, there should be a stronger family focus and youth involvement and support. The training and research funds designated in this Act should be considered for use to train teachers, related services professionals, and parents to recognize signs of emotional and behavioral problems in children, make appropriate referrals for assessment and services and classroom accommodations, and implement and evaluate evidence-based school mental health interventions.

On a related topic, the Commission recognizes the particular challenges for youth in transition from adolescence to adulthood. IDEA has transition requirements beginning at age 14, but to date, these requirements have not resulted in acceptable post-school outcomes.

Studies show that approximately 42% of students with serious emotional disturbances graduate from high school as opposed to 57% of students with other disabilities. Schools and local mental health agencies could improve their collaboration and use of evidence-based practices to develop transition-to-work services so that children with serious emotional disorders can move successfully from school to employment or to post-secondary education.

| *"Coerced mental health screening pro-grams have no place in a free society."*

Government-Sponsored Mental Health Screenings Would Not Benefit Children

Phyllis Schlafly

In the following viewpoint Phyllis Schlafly argues against the U.S. government's plan to launch mandatory mental health screenings for all public school students. Such a plan is unconstitutional, Schlafly contends, because it takes away parents' rights to care for their own children. Moreover, the inaccuracy of mental health screenings could lead to false diagnoses and the misguided use of potentially dangerous psychiatric medications, she explains. There is also a danger that authorities could use mental health screenings to enforce social conformity and political correctness among children, Schlafly warns. Author and commentator Phyllis Schlafly is the founder of the Eagle Forum, a conservative political organization.

As you read, consider the following questions:

1. Why does Schlafly object to the questions children are asked on Columbia University's "TeenScreen" mental health questionnaire?

Phyllis Schlafly, "No Child Left Unmedicated," *Phyllis Schlafly Report*, vol. 38, no. 8, March 2005. Reproduced by permission.

2. According to the author, why is it difficult to diagnose mental illness in children?

3. What side effects can psychiatric medications have in children, according to Schlafly?

Big Brother is on the march. A plan to subject all children to mental health screening is underway, and the pharmaceutical corporations are gearing up for bigger sales of antidepressant and psychostimulant drugs.

Like most liberal big-spending ideas, this one was slipped into the law under cover of sweet words. It started with the New Freedom Commission on Mental Health created by President George W. Bush's Executive Order 13263 of April 29, 2002. The Commission issued its report on July 22, 2003. President Bush has instructed 25 federal agencies to develop a plan to implement the Commission's recommendations.

In 2004, Congress appropriated $20 million to finance the recommendations of this New Freedom Commission on Mental Health. Congress also passed the Garrett Lee Smith Memorial Act that included $7 million for suicide screening, and tens of millions more for the Substance Abuse and Mental Health Services Administration and its Center for Mental Health Services. The No Child Left Behind Act already includes $5 million for Mental Health Integration. These funds appear to be part of a larger plan to get more and more people labeled and in the psychiatric system or, as some say, to move children into the psychotherapeutic state.

Forced Psychiatric Screenings

This Commission on Mental Health laid out a federal plan that could subject all children to mental health screening in school and during routine physical exams. The clear plan is to use the public schools to subject all children to mental examinations, forcing millions of kids to undergo psychiatric screening whether their parents consent or not. The Commission report states on page 58:

"Schools must be partners in the mental health care of our children. Schools are in a key position to identify mental health problems early and to provide a link to appropriate services. Every day more than 52 million students attend over 114,000 schools in the U.S. When combined with the six million adults working at those schools, almost one-fifth of the population passes through the nation's schools on any given weekday."

The Commission wants "routine and comprehensive" testing and mental health screening of every child in America, including preschoolers. The Commission recommends "linkage" of these mental examinations with "state-of-the-art treatments" using "specific medications for specific conditions." That means prescribing more expensive patented antidepressants and psychostimulant drugs such as Ritalin. Children's mental health data will be entered into state and federal computer databases and integrated with the child's other health and education records.

Perks from Drug Companies

The New Freedom Commission on Mental Health praised the Texas Algorithm Project as a "model" medication treatment plan. It advocates the use of newer, more expensive antidepressants and antipsychotic drugs. But when Allen Jones, an employee of the Pennsylvania Office of Inspector General, revealed that key officials with influence over the medication plan in his state received money and perks from the drug companies, he was fired for talking to the *New York Times*.

Parental rights are unclear or non-existent under these mental screening programs. Parental rights can depend on who pays for the screening programs, which budgets are used, and who is implementing the programs. Federal consent protections that exist in the Department of Education do not apply if the programs come from Health and Human Services or from a private foundation or university. Even if there are limited protections, the Nanny State and its allies in the mental health community can find ways around them.

What are the rights of youth and parents to refuse or opt out of mental screening? Will they face coercion and threats of removal from school, or child neglect charges, if they refuse privacy-invading interrogations or unproved medications? How will a child remove a stigmatizing label from his records? We don't know the answers to these questions.

TeenScreen

The government bureaucrats who are promoting universal mental health screening for all children are praising a Columbia University–based program called TeenScreen as a national model. This program has already been tried out on 43,000 young people in 36 states. It screens 9th- and 10th-graders for risk of suicide, anxiety disorders, depression, and drug and alcohol disorders.

Columbia University put millions into developing and piloting TeenScreen, but won't say where the funding came from. Leslie McGuire, director of the TeenScreen Program, stated: "Our goal is to get every child in America a mental health check-up before leaving high school."

Here are some of the very nosy questions that TeenScreen has been asking children:

- "Have you often felt very nervous or uncomfortable when you have been with a group of children or young people, say, like in the lunchroom at school or at a party?

- Have you often felt very nervous when you've had things to do in front of people?

- Has there been a time when nothing was fun for you and you just weren't interested in anything?

- Has there been a time when you had less energy than you usually do?

• Has there been a time when you felt you couldn't do anything well or that you weren't as good-looking or as smart as other people?"

It's easy to see that many teens would honestly answer Yes to those questions, but that certainly doesn't prove they are crazy or even that they have mental health problems. Nosy questionnaires are very intimidating to many students and their parents, and such use has been a matter of legislation and litigation for several decades.

TeenScreen officials, however, claim that up to one-third of the students who undergo screening show some signs of mental health problems, and about half of those are referred to receive mental health services. That means about 15% of the students screened are labeled as having mental health problems, and their treatment can and often does lead toward the use of powerful and sometimes dangerous medications.

It is truly shocking that government employees or others can ask children those ridiculous questions, use them as a basis for deciding whether a child has mental problems, and then refer the kids to mental health providers who are eager to prescribe drugs. It is vitally important that parents insist on prior parental consent before their children are subjected to any mental health screening or to nosy psychological questionnaires, surveys or tests by the government, the schools, private foundations, or universities. . . .

Subjective and Unreliable

It is bad enough that federal and state governments are involved in any way in determining the mental health of their citizens, but to make matters worse the criteria used by the psychiatric and psychological community to determine a diagnosis of mental illness are subjective, culturally biased, and unreliable. Even the so-called experts admit that mental health diagnoses are inherently subjective.

The 1999 Surgeon General's report on mental health admitted that there are serious conflicts in medical literature about the definitions of mental health and mental illness. The very definitions are rooted in value judgments that vary across cultures.

The diagnosis of mental illness is far more difficult and in many cases impossible, as compared to the diagnosis of medical disorders. The former is based on behaviors as observed by others and subjective reporting, while the latter is based on objectively verifiable physical signs.

Mental illness diagnoses are especially difficult for children because the normal child is developing so rapidly and doesn't stay the same long enough to make stable measurements. The diagnostic criteria are vague. Because of inherent subjectivity and lack of objective verification, its all too easy for a psychiatrist to label disagreement with political and/or social beliefs to be a mental disorder.

Leftist Social Workers

We also have to be concerned about social workers who play a major role in many families' lives, especially as more and more family functions are taken over by the school and state. Many social workers and other similarly trained mental health-care practitioners have been trained mostly in post-modern sociology and leftist ideology. This can give them built-in biases against gun ownership, homeschoolers, discipline, spanking, parental rights, extended families, and what they consider overemphasis on religion and morality.

More and more physicians are asking questions about family gun ownership as part of routine health examinations. When mental health screening is integrated with academic reports, it becomes very easy to go over the line into judging deviations from political correctness as symptoms of some kind of mental disorder.

Little Evidence of Suicide Prevention

Not only are the diagnostic criteria vague and subjective and some peoples motivations questionable, but even one of the stated purposes of mental health screening programs—to prevent suicide—has been shown to be useless and perhaps even counterproductive.

The U.S. Preventive Services Task Force reported that it "found no evidence that screening for suicide risk reduces suicide attempts or mortality. There is limited evidence on the accuracy of screening tools to identify suicide risk in the primary care setting, including tools to identify those at high risk."

The diagnostic criteria and screening instruments are problematic and some researchers now say that the antidepressant drugs are no better than placebos in alleviating depressive symptoms in children and teens. Nevertheless, in 2002, the last year for which total figures are available, doctors wrote nearly 11 million prescriptions for antidepressants to teenagers and children.

Antidepressants don't provide any long-term improvement in academic achievement, athletic skills, social skills, or reduced anti-social behavior. At best, they offer short-term assistance; at worst they hide the actual problems and contribute to them.

Dangers of Psychiatric Drugs

Then there is Attention Deficit Disorder (ADD) and the psychostimulants used for its treatment. The criteria used for diagnosing ADD are notoriously subjective, and over-diagnosis is believed to be widespread.

Recent research at Harvard Medical Schools McLean Hospital and the University of Texas-Southwestern has reported depressive symptoms in rats that are exposed to Ritalin early in life. These findings raise concerns that Ritalin and other stimulants used to treat Attention Deficit Disorder in young children may permanently alter the brain and lead to depression in adulthood. One of the findings of this work is that the effect of Ritalin doesn't go away as the child grows up.

We face the additional problem that the long-term safety and effectiveness of psychiatric medications on children have never been proven. The side effects of some suggested medications in children can be severe. They include suicide, violence, psychosis, cardiac toxicity, and growth suppression. That sounds like a list of everything bad that can happen.

Nevertheless, we have seen a tremendous increase in the prescription of psychiatric drugs to children. We've had a 300% increase in psychotropic drugs for 2-, 3-, and 4-year-olds. Several school shooters, including Eric Harris (Columbine) and Kip Kinkel (Oregon) were on antidepressants or stimulants or both at the time of their crimes.

FDA Supervision?

In 2004, the Food and Drug Administration finally responded to public pressure to warn against risks associated with antidepressants given to minors. In October, the FDA ordered that all antidepressants must carry "black box" warnings saying that antidepressants "increase the risk of suicidal thinking and behavior" in children who take them. The FDA's action, which followed a recommendation of its advisory panel, was the result of data showing that, on average, 2% to 3% of children taking antidepressants have *increased* thoughts about suicide.

The FDA decision came some ten months after regulators in England declared that most antidepressants are not suitable for children under 18.

The pharmaceutical companies exercise a powerful influence on the studies and on the approval process of various drugs. The FDA finally announced in 2005 that persons who receive pay or perks from the pharmaceutical companies may not serve on panels that approve the drugs.

Under universal screening programs, any thousands if not millions of children could receive stigmatizing diagnoses that could handicap them for the rest of their lives. "State-of-the-art treatments" will result in many thousands of children being medicated by expensive, ineffective, and often even dangerous drugs. It is unclear what effect the FDA decision will have on the Mental Health Commission's stated desire to increase the availability of pharmaceutical options to schoolchildren.

Parents' Rights

The real issue is the fundamental right of parents to decide what medical treatment is appropriate for their own children. Coerced mental health screening programs have no place in a free society. Neither does coerced medication. The government does not own you or your children, and it has no legitimate authority to interfere in your family's intimate health matters.

Since we also know that psychiatric diagnoses are inherently subjective, and the drugs usually prescribed to treat so-called mental illnesses can produce serious side effects, we need to be even more concerned with these types of government programs.

Unfortunately, we have too many examples of parents being coerced to give psychotropic drugs to their children. This happened even before any universal mental health screening programs have been implemented statewide. The parents can be and have been threatened that they cannot send their child to school, or even that child protective services will take their child away, if they do not give the child the ordered psychotropic drug. Tragic examples include Matthew Smith and Shaina Dunkle who died of medication toxicity after their parents were coerced into placing their children on drugs by the schools. . . .

What's Wrong with Mental Health Screening?

First, the plan is unconstitutional because it overrides parents' rights to the care and control of their own children. After all, who owns the children, parents or the government?

Second, mental diagnoses are subjective, and this is admitted by the experts. There is no scientific agreement on the definition of mental health or of mental illness.

Third, mental diagnoses are even less scientific for children. The younger the child, the less accurate is any diagnosis because a normal child is constantly changing.

Fourth, medications are already over-prescribed and children over-medicated even though medications don't usually work on children, the medications have not been tested on children or tested for long-term effects, and there are numerous examples of medications causing suicide, death or crimes.

Fifth, suicide prevention is given as a major reason for mental screening, but there is no evidence that mental screening or medications or school courses prevent suicide.

Sixth, mental screening results in stigmatizing children with a label that may be false, that is impossible to erase from his record, and that may handicap him as an adult (such as preventing him from joining the Armed Services, getting some types of jobs, or buying a gun).

Seventh, universal mental screening presents a real danger that the schools or the child protection agency may coerce parents to submit their kids to mental interrogation, screening, treatment or education under threat of retaliation.

Eighth, there is a real danger that universal mental screening will be used for politically motivated purposes, to identify and change the attitudes of children whose religious or social views may not be politically correct.

Periodical Bibliography

The following articles have been selected to supplement the diverse views presented in this chapter.

Sharon Begley — "Why Depression Looks Different in a Kid's Brain," *Wall Street Journal*, October 15, 2004.

Carolyn Kleiner Butler — "The Pressure Mounts," *U.S. News and World Report*, April 11, 2005.

B.K. Eakman — "Mandatory Mental Health Screenings: A Threat to Every Parent and Child," *Practical Homeschooling*, May/June 2005.

Douglas J. Edwards — "When Kids' Only 'Crime' Is Having a Mental Illness," *Behavioral Health Management*, July/August 2005.

Lee Gomes — "Smart, Robotic Toys May One Day Diagnose Autism at Early Age," *Wall Street Journal*, October 26, 2005.

Jane Gross — "As Autistic Children Grow, So Does Social Gap," *New York Times*, February 26, 2005.

Robin Marantz Henig — "Sorry. Your Eating Disorder Doesn't Meet Our Criteria," *New York Times*, November 30, 2004.

Jonathan Mahler — "The Antidepressant Dilemma," *New York Times Magazine*, November 21, 2004.

Daniel McGinn and Ron Depasquale — "Taking Depression On," *Newsweek*, August 23, 2004.

Walt Mueller — "See the Signs," *youthculture@today*, Summer 2005. www.cpyu.org.

Shari Roan — "After Drug Scare, No Easy Answers for Depressed Kids," *Los Angeles Times*, March 21, 2005.

Michele G. Sullivan — "Higher Prevalence of Autism Is Real, Expert Says," *Family Practice News*, May 1, 2005.

CHAPTER 4

What Treatments
for Mental Illness
Are Effective?

Chapter Preface

During the past twenty years there has been a proliferation of increasingly effective psychiatric drugs. With the recognition that many mental illnesses are associated with chemical imbalances in the brain, improved medications for depression, obsessive-compulsive disorder, anxiety, and schizophrenia have been made available to the afflicted. As Steven Hyman of the National Institute of Mental Health notes, "Today the psychiatrists who treat patients are working hand in hand with the 'wet-brain guys'—the pharmacologists, chemists and molecular biologists."

These scientists have uncovered the biochemical processes that correspond to thoughts, emotions, moods, and memories. Neuron (nerve cell) receptors—which are specific kinds of protein molecules—and the substances that connect with them play a crucial role in brain activity. As an electrical signal moves from nerve cell to nerve cell, it must cross a small space, the synapse, between the cells. A variety of brain chemicals known as neurotransmitters carry these signals across the synapse and then bind to the receptors on other nerve cells. Thus, brain cells communicate with one another through the work of neurotransmitters and receptors. With their increasingly refined understanding of brain biochemistry, pharmacologists are able to create drugs that bind to specific neural receptors by mimicking the action of certain neurotransmitters. In doing so, drug designers can counteract the symptoms of many mental disorders, offering patients welcome relief.

Many people approach psychoactive drugs with caution, however. Jodi Jensen, a communications professor at the University of Tulsa who suffers from occasional depression, feels skeptical about the constant promotion and marketing of antidepressants. She relates:

Plenty of experts have tried to convince me that I need mood medication. In the last 10 years my primary care physician, my gynecologist, and even my allergist's assistant have offered to get me prescriptions. I'm also being targeted by pharmaceutical companies with magazine and TV ads that describe me exactly and tell me that I can greet the dawn with gusto, romp with my children, smile at myself in the mirror, and be productive, cheerful, and optimistic ("like myself again") if I take their drugs.

Jensen, however, resists taking mood medications because she thinks that they often create drug dependencies in people. She prefers to find nondrug ways to manage her depressive tendencies. "My moodiness is—and has always been—my 'self.' Perhaps there's some benefit to living with, rather than medicating, my temperament."

While many psychotherapists agree that medication can help alleviate the symptoms of mental disorders, they warn against viewing psychiatric drugs as a "magic bullet" that can cure illness. Depression, for example, may be rooted in underlying psychological problems, not biochemistry. Thus, talk therapy—with or without drug therapy—is often needed to treat depression because it teaches people the life skills that they need to prevent further recurrences of the disorder.

Whether the treatment of mental illness should be approached through drug or nondrug therapies—or a combination of both—largely depends on the severity of the disorder and individual preference. In the following chapter authors examine the efficacy of several treatments for mental illness, including electroconvulsive therapy, cognitive behavioral therapy, and acceptance therapy.

> "[Electroconvulsive therapy] can be a
> very effective treatment for a poten-
> tially life-threatening condition."

Electroconvulsive Therapy Can Be Effective

Val Flint

*In the following viewpoint Val Flint asserts that electroconvulsive
therapy (ECT)—in which electricity is sent through electrodes
that have been placed on a patient's head—is an effective treatment for people suffering from serious mental disturbances. Flint
discusses the case of a patient suffering from catatonia, a mo-
tionless, apathetic, and uncommunicative state that can result
from severe depression. After eight sessions of ECT, the patient
had greatly improved and was able to return home to a relatively normal life. Flint concludes that ECT is re-emerging as a
safe treatment for certain disorders. Flint is a registered nurse
who specializes in mental health services.*

As you read, consider the following questions:

1. How does popular culture tend to portray ECT, according to Flint?

Val Flint, "The Place of ECT in Mental Health Care," *Kai Tiaki: Nursing New Zealand*,
vol. 11, no. 9, October 2005, pp. 18–19. Copyright © 2005 New Zealand Nurses Organisation. Reproduced by permission.

2. How was the patient Trevor treated during his first ECT treatment?

3. How did Trevor score on the Montgomery and Asberg Depression Rating Scale after his three-week series of ECT treatments?

Electroconvulsive therapy (ECT) is one of the most controversial treatments in medicine. It has a chequered history of misuse and abuse. Some of those who recall having had unmodified ECT, i.e. without anaesthetic or muscle relaxant, retain nightmare memories of the treatment. Some people remember being given ECT as a punishment for perceived poor behaviour, or to coerce them to conform to acceptable "normal" behaviours. In 2001, 95 people who had been patients in Lake Alice Hospital near Wanganui, [New Zealand,] received $6.5 million in compensation for the abuse they suffered. Many who received compensation had been given unmodified shock treatment, and when describing their experiences today, they use the term "torture" in relation to ECT. Popular culture has tended to portray the procedure and outcomes of ECT negatively. Many people's understanding of the treatment is based on the 1975 film, *One Flew over the Cuckoo's Nest*. Seldom does one read or hear of the positive effects of ECT for those who present with a life-threatening mental disorder. An exception was an article published in the *New Zealand Listener* in 2003. This presented evidence and views from experts both in favour of, and against ECT.

An Effective Treatment for Catatonia

Electroconvulsive therapy is no longer used indiscriminately, as was the case in the 1950s and 1960s. It has proven to be an effective treatment for catatonia and catatonic states. [According to eMedicine.com,] "Catatonia is a state of apparent unresponsiveness to external stimuli in a person who is apparently awake, and is difficult to differentiate from diffuse encephalopathy [brain disease] and non-convulsive status epilepticus [continuous seizures]. . . . Diagnostic criteria for catatonia include motoric immobility, excessive motor activity, extreme negativism or mutism, peculiarities of voluntary movement, and echolalia or echopraxia [repeating the words or actions of others, respectively]." Two of these symptoms are required to diagnose catatonia in schizophrenia and mood disorder. Only one is required to diagnose catatonia in general medical conditions. Catatonia can present in an immobile state (apparently stuporose) and is potentially life-threatening, unless nutrition is administered parenterally [non-orally].

Extreme excitability in a catatonic state presents a risk of injuring self and/or others, with ensuing autonomic disturbances, such as tachycardia [fast heart rate] and hypertension [high blood pressure], and can result in collapse. Catatonia is not related to any specific age group or gender. Children as young as eight have received ECT to relieve them of this condition when all other treatments have failed.

A Case Study in ECT Use

I was closely involved in caring for a client for whom ECT treatment for catatonia was successful. Trevor (not his real name) had no previous-known psychiatric disorder and there was no family history of mental ill health. Trevor had experienced a traumatic incident at work. During the following four weeks his mood progressively deteriorated, with a decrease in responsiveness and activity. He presented to a medical ward in a severe catatonic state, resistive to physical examination, adamantly but mutely refusing to open his eyes or mouth, and combative when nurses attempted to reposition him.

To eliminate other diagnoses, the patient underwent a thorough medical and physical investigation but nothing abnormal was discovered. These investigations included a chest x-ray; an electrocardiograph; a full blood screen; lumbar puncture for cerebral-spinal fluid abnormality; a CAT brain scan; a magnetic resonance imaging brain scan; electroencephalo-

The Benefits of Electroconvulsive Therapy

Duke University psychiatry professor Richard Wiener, M.D., an authority on ECT, has stated that, according to meta-analytic studies (studies whose conclusions stem from statistically combining data from many studies), the likelihood that ECT is more effective against depression than are antidepressants is 99.99 percent. (A probability of 95 percent is usually considered adequate for deciding whether one modality is better than another.) In 1987 the American Psychiatric Association (APA) appointed Wiener to chair a task force on ECT. The task force concluded that ECT was effective not only against depression but also against mania (a condition marked by overstimulation and a lack of judgment and self-control), bipolar disorder (manic depression), and some types of schizophrenia. The APA endorsed its conclusions in 1990.

Rael Jean Isaac, Priorities for Health, *vol. 11, No. 1, 1999.*

graph; thyroid function tests; toxicology screening; and syphilis serology. He was given intravenous (IV) fluids for nutrition, as he was not taking any food or drink. He resisted oral cares, clenching his jaws tightly. A neurology review showed no evidence of any neurological disorder.

A referral was sent to the mental health team for an assessment of his mental health status. Since delirium had been ruled out, a diagnosis of a catatonic state was made. Because Trevor had no previous psychiatric history, a definitive diagnosis of catatonic schizophrenia could not be established. The mental health team advised ECT, as this has been used successfully to treat catatonia, "effectively releasing the patient from an apparent state of stupor to one of recovery and the resumption of a normal active life" [as reported on mhsource.com].

Next of kin or other family members cannot give consent for ECT and, as Trevor was not able to give informed consent for the treatment, he was placed under the Mental Health Act (MHA) Section 11. This is a five-day compulsory assessment and treatment order and ECT is prescribed and administered under section 60(b) of the MHA. A second opinion from a suitably appointed psychiatrist must be sought and assessment conducted and recorded using a particular legal form.

The ECT nurse plays a crucial role in all issues involving the administration of ECT. She is a co-ordinator, an educator, she liaises [acts as a link] with other services and families, and is a point of contact about ECT within the mental health service generally and in the ECT unit in particular.

The Family Is Informed

The nurse caring for Trevor on the medical ward contacted the ECT nurse for information regarding the treatment and the MHA. This was provided in as much detail as was required. The family had been fully informed of the proposed treatment, the risks involved, potential side-effects and the anticipated benefits. The family was given a comprehensive information booklet about ECT and was invited to ask any questions in relation to the treatment. The family was satisfied with the information and agreed that Trevor should receive ECT.

Escorted by his nurse and the ECT nurse, Trevor was taken from the medical ward in his bed to the ECT suite for his first three treatments. In the suite he was greeted warmly by the ECT team and was given step-by-step verbal information about the procedure, despite his apparent semi-comatose state. The ECT nurse remained with him, holding his hand by way of reassurance, while the anaesthetist and the psychiatrist explained to Trevor exactly what they were doing. Trevor recovered quickly from the ECT treatment, with no untoward events and was returned to the medical ward. Response after the first

ECT treatment was minimal but evident. Trevor was able to specify which drink he wanted when his nurse asked him to nod or shake his head to indicate what drink he wanted. He accepted sips of water and co-operated with mouth cares; however he continued to refuse to eat or to open his eyes.

After the second ECT treatment his condition showed little improvement, although Trevor did continue to comply with oral cares and accept fluids. Naso-gastric feeding [through a tube inserted into the nose and down into the stomach] was to be considered if his nutritional intake did not improve after the third ECT treatment.

The Turning Point

The third treatment proved to be the turning point. In the recovery room, Trevor opened his eyes. He was wheeled back to the medical ward where he ate a full breakfast. He was able to respond verbally and later got up from his bed to walk quite steadily around the ward. The mental health team conducted a further assessment and agreed that Trevor could be transferred from the medical ward to the mental health unit, as he no longer required intensive medical and nursing cares.

During an interview in the mental health unit with a psychiatrist and a mental health primary nurse, Trevor denied any thoughts of self-harm or suicide and said he was feeling slightly better. Despite this, he appeared low in mood, his responses were restricted, poverty of thought and speech were evident, and he made only fleeting eye contact. He spoke in a quiet monotone and was extremely retarded [slow] in his responses to questions, appearing somewhat preoccupied and guarded throughout the interview. There was evidence of paranoia, as he intimated that people were talking about him and putting him down in relation to the incident at work. He denied any alcohol or illegal substance abuse. He indicated that his family was extremely supportive and anxious for his recovery and return home. Trevor was fully orientated to time, place and person but was hesitant in his responses, apparently unable to concentrate on the questions being asked.

A Course of ECT

The plan was for Trevor to continue with a course of ECT and to commence anti-depressants. His primary nurse was responsible for gathering information from other members of the team, including occupational and art therapists, and for recording and reporting these and her findings to the multi-disciplinary team. Trevor was to be observed for any psychotic features; his food and fluid intake and his ability with activities of daily living (ADL) were to be monitored. Participation in ward social activities was to be encouraged and family contact maintained.

Over the next three weeks, Trevor received a total of eight ECT treatments and improved with each treatment. On the ward Trevor continued to look preoccupied at times but stated he was "thinking" when asked about this by his nurse. His family had described Trevor as a shy, introspective young man, who had no special relationships outside the family circle, so he was assessed as being naturally quiet. However, he gradually became less isolated, joined others in spontaneous group activities, as well as organised group work, and his appetite improved to the point where he looked forward to meals and wanted snacks in between. Trevor went home to his family on leave twice and on his return to the ward reported that all had gone well.

Just before his discharge, the ECT nurse made an appointment with Trevor and his primary nurse to conduct an assessment of his level of depression, using the revised version of the Montgomery and Asberg Depression Rating Scale (MADRAS). This is a ten-point questionnaire with ratings of 0–6 on nine questions and 0–5 on one question, with the higher number indicating the most severe depression. Trevor scored five out of a potential 59, which signified minimal depression. During the assessment he appeared a little sad and made little eye contact. He reported occasional feelings of anxiety; poor sleep at times; occasional difficulties with concentrating; and some sluggishness when having to embark on his ADLs. Due to Trevor's initial catatonic state it had not been possible to conduct a baseline assessment before ECT started, therefore there was no way of comparing the severity of his depression pre- and post-treatment. Trevor was discharged home with a minor depression which did not interfere with his normal functioning and he was showing signs of enjoying [life] once again.

An Accepted Practice

Despite the adverse publicity ECT has received, in the past decade it has re-emerged as a safe and effective treatment for major depressive disorders, with the greatest interest in research and use being in the United States (US). It is an accepted part of psychiatric practice in the Scandinavian countries, Great Britain, Ireland, Australia and New Zealand, and use is similar to that in the US.

As the case study of Trevor demonstrates, ECT can be a very effective treatment for a potentially life-threatening condition.

"Those who do feel better after a series of shocks almost always plunge back into depression within a few weeks, or months."

The Results of Electroconvulsive Therapy Are Unpredictable

Benedict Carey

Although electroconvulsive therapy (ECT) has regained acceptance as a treatment for severe depression, its results remain unreliable, reports Benedict Carey in the following viewpoint. Today ECT is administered in a more refined and precise way, and it does not cause the bodily convulsions seen with older versions of "shock therapy," Carey notes. Patients who show initial improvements after an ECT treatment, however, often relapse into serious depression weeks or months later. In addition, many ECT patients experience memory loss. Researchers are still not sure whether ECT ultimately enhances brain function or causes brain damage. Carey is a staff writer for the Los Angeles Times.

As you read, consider the following questions:

1. Since the 1990s, how many people have been treated with ECT per year, according to the author?

Benedict Carey, "Shock Therapy and the Brain," *Los Angeles Times*, November 17, 2003, p. F1. Reproduced by permission.

2. According to Carey, how did shock therapy emerge as a treatment for mental illness?

3. What kind of biological effects does ECT have on the brain, according to the author?

The electrical current throbs from one side of the skull to the other, scrambling circuits along the way, inducing a brief seizure. When it's over and the anesthesia wears off, patients often are subdued, confused, sometimes unsure of where they are or why. Then, sometimes, the remarkable happens: Severely depressed people feel better than they have in years. Others are left distraught. They feel no better than before.

In recent years, electroconvulsive therapy, or ECT, has undergone a transformation, many psychiatrists say. The body no longer thrashes violently, as depicted in movies a generation ago; it lies still, under medication, with the thrashing confined to the mind. Techniques are more precise, they say; the brain better understood.

Although exact numbers are not available on how many people get modern ECT—estimates have ranged from 30,000 to more than 50,000 a year since the early 1990s—scientific interest in the treatment has surged, in part because of the acknowledgment that drugs don't help many deeply depressed people, particularly older adults, a growing and hard-to-treat population. The government is funding some 20 ECT studies to see how different techniques and treatment combinations affect behavior.

Altering Biology

Recently, researchers have looked directly at how the bolts of current alter biology, by studying the brains of shocked rodents. And in June [2003], a leading medical journal published the results of a broad survey detailing what former ECT patients think about the treatment.

Yet far from proving the effectiveness of ECT, the emerging research has only accentuated its unknowns and shortcomings. After more than 60 years of experience, doctors still don't know exactly how the shocks affect the brain, whether they cause permanent damage, or why they affect depression. Although the techniques and technology have improved, ECT itself appears no more effective than it ever was, studies show.

When it comes to treating older people in particular, doctors have no scientifically rigorous evidence establishing the treatment's safety or effectiveness, according to an exhaustive review of the literature published [in October 2003]. "Proponents have been saying it's safe and effective, but their statements go beyond what we know for elderly people," said John Bola, a mental health researcher at USC [the University of Southern California] who studies treatment effectiveness. "It starts to sound more like an advertisement than a statement of fact."

The Reputation of Shock Therapy

The reputation of therapy has alternately risen and fallen since 1938, when an Italian psychiatrist named Ugo Cerletti decided to try shocking one of his patients, a 39-year-old man, after watching slaughterhouse workers subdue pigs with bolts of current delivered to the brain, and after first experimenting on animals. Cerletti reported that the man improved after repeated shocks, and the idea soon caught on among doctors desperate for some way to manage disturbed, often aggressive, patients. Use of the treatment then declined through the 1960s and 1970s, due to the introduction of new psychiatric drugs and the public stigma attached to the therapy.

That decline stopped in the 1980s, researchers say, because psychiatrists refined their techniques and continued to report recoveries in severely depressed people who didn't respond to any other treatment. By 1990, an American Psychiatric Assn. task force report on ECT concluded that the treatment was highly effective, "with 80% to 90% of those treated showing improvement." The association also set precise guidelines for treatment, specifying the amounts of electricity and placement of electrodes that seemed to produce the best results.

"You're talking about people who are desperate, who are often suicidal, who have just about lost it all," said psychologist Harold Sackeim, chief of biological psychiatry at the New York State Psychiatric Institute and a professor at Columbia and Cornell universities in New York. "This is a treatment that we know can help them turn it around, and it is very satisfying to see that happen."

Relief Is Usually Temporary

Psychiatrists acknowledge that the mood-altering effect of ECT is usually very short-lived: Those who do feel better after a series of shocks almost always plunge back into depression within a few weeks or months. Aggressively treating these people with drugs can help; but it is hardly a guarantee that the depression will lift, or that a person will agree to endure such treatment in the first place.

"It must be thought of as a stopgap measure in life-threatening situations," said Dr. Jeffrey Schwartz, a research psychiatrist at UCLA's Neuropsychiatric Institute. "All you're doing is buying more time to get to a place where drugs, or cognitive therapy, can have some effect."

In an article in the March 14, 2001, *Journal of the American Medical Assn.*, researchers at Columbia University in New York reported that a combination of ECT and aggressive drug treatment successfully vanquished depression in 14 of 23 people (61%) for at least six months. This is a significant improvement, and far more effective than ECT alone, which helped only four of 25 people in the study (16%) for six months.

But the researchers also reported that more than half of the 316 people originally enrolled and given shock therapy dropped out of the study, or were excluded. Most of these people didn't feel at all better after the shocks, others refused further treatment; and some suffered medical complications. The success rate of the treatments is based only on the fraction of the people who both responded well to the shock and had no adverse reactions or second thoughts. Without continual therapy of some kind, the authors conclude, "almost universal relapse should be expected."

"Maintenance" Shock Therapy

Some psychiatrists believe that the solution for this is more ECT. Continuation-ECT, or C-ECT, as it's known, involves "maintenance" shock sessions every three to six months, or whatever seems best suited to the patient. Some psychiatrists have been providing C-ECT for years, and hundreds of people are already on this steady regimen, experts estimate.

Yet there's no scientifically rigorous evidence that continually shocking a person is safe, and it could cause damage, some doctors say.

In several recent studies in rats, scientists have reported some of the first direct evidence of biological changes from the treatments that might be related to changes in behavior. They report that ECT accelerates the production of new brain cells in these animals and spurs the growth of neural connections called mossy fibers. Some ECT doctors say new neurons are probably helpful and that new nerve connections may enhance brain function.

"These changes could help explain how it is that these severely depressed patients recover," said Dr. Sarah Lisanby, a Columbia University psychiatrist who heads the American Psychiatric Assn.'s ECT Committee.

Lisanby acknowledges, though, that doctors aren't sure whether the brain changes are good or bad. The studies purporting to show brain cell proliferation due to ECT may in fact be showing evidence of brain cell damage, according to Richard Nowakowski, a neuroscientist at the Robert Wood

Johnson School of Medicine in Piscataway, N.J., who pioneered the use of the cellular techniques used in the experiments. "It's not clear in these studies whether they're seeing proliferation or something else," he said. As far as what the changes actually mean, he said, "anyone who tells you they know doesn't."

Nor is it clear what the growth of these new neural connections means. Neuroscientists say that the brain's nerve networks are laid down over years, as the brain develops and responds to the outside world. The chances that an instantaneous, shock-induced fiber would make exactly the right connections to enhance function, they say, are extremely remote. Moreover, the kind of neural sprouting, or mossy fiber proliferation, observed in shocked animals also turns up in the brains of people who have epilepsy, a neurological disease in which the body suffers periodic, unexplained seizures. "In this area, there's a debate over whether the epilepsy causes the fibers, or the fibers cause the epilepsy," said Nowakowski.

Patients' Reactions Vary

The men and women on the receiving end of the electrodes vary widely in their judgment of the effect. Some are grateful for the treatment, and insist that the shocks both relieved their illness and improved their cognitive function. Others are outraged. Over the years, the practice of ECT has spawned a large and vocal group of critics who say the shocks harmed them, mainly by erasing memory.

"There are thousands of people out there who feel they weren't told the whole story before getting the treatment," said Juli Lawrence, 44, a St. Louis–based freelance writer who started the Web site ect.org after a series of shock treatments failed to lift her depression and obliterated about two years of memory.

In the first large-scale effort to learn from ECT patients themselves, researchers in England reviewed 35 studies of patient attitudes. All told, the studies involved more than 2,000 men and women who got ECT treatment in the last two decades or earlier. Depending on the study, 30% to 80% of former patients reported lasting memory loss. In one survey, a third of patients agreed with the statement, "Electroconvulsive therapy permanently wipes out large parts of memory." The proportion of people who considered the treatment ultimately helpful varied just as widely—from about one-third, when patients helped design or conduct surveys, to about three-fourths, when doctors did.

"This is what happens when you ask patients what they think," said patient-turned-prominent-ECT-critic Linda Andre, who has questioned ECT research and practice. "You get a completely different story from the one psychiatrists are telling."

Weighing Benefits and Risks

Dr. Loren Mosher, former director of schizophrenia research at the National Institute of Mental Health and now a clinical professor of psychiatry at UC San Diego, said the issue comes down to a "cost-benefit" analysis. "Does it make sense to expose people to something which not only isn't very effective but also has serious inherent danger? In my view, the cost to the person is greater than the potential benefit."

Until doctors find an answer for severe depression whose costs are not so steep, the controversy is not likely to diminish. Drug companies have been working to find better antidepressants for years, so far without significantly improving on what's been available for the last 10 years or so. Now, Lisanby and other researchers are investigating the possibility of using magnetically induced convulsions as an alternative to electricity. A strong magnetic field near the head can also induce a brief seizure. The hope is that the magnetic stimulation might "break" the depression in the same way ECT does, but for longer than a few months or weeks and without the memory loss.

"ECT is an important treatment, and has helped to save the lives of many patients, many of my own patients, but we need to do better, to find treatments that are more tolerable and accessible," Lisanby said.

In order to determine safety and side effects, doctors at Columbia and the New York State Psychiatric Institute induced brain seizures in 10 severely depressed men and women with bursts of magnetic stimulation. They report that these shocks induced fewer memory problems than ECT.

As for the effect on depression, psychiatrists in Europe have reported on one person who got a full treatment course of magnetic shocks. A 20-year-old woman, she felt an almost immediate lifting of her mood, according to psychological measures done after the treatment.

But to prevent relapse, doctors decided she needed further treatment—with ECT.

"So much that we do in life has to do with attitude, expectations, and, ultimately, choice."

Schizophrenics Can Choose to Cure Themselves

Elizabeth A. Richter

Schizophrenia—a serious mental disorder characterized by disorganized thinking, delusions, and hallucinations—is not necessarily incurable, writes Elizabeth A. Richter in the following viewpoint. She notes that 25 percent of patients diagnosed with schizophrenia recover spontaneously, without therapy. Richter herself was hospitalized with schizophrenia years ago, and although she has occasionally taken medication, she would not be classified as schizophrenic today. She believes that she chose to get well and that others who have the potential to recover should be encouraged to make this choice. Richter is a freelance writer in Canton, Connecticut.

As you read, consider the following questions:

1. What did a mental health worker tell Richter during her hospitalization for schizophrenia?

Elizabeth A. Richter, "My Schizophrenia," *Liberty*, vol. 17, no. 1, January 2003, pp. 39–40. Copyright © 2006 Liberty Foundation. Reproduced by permission.

2. According to the author, how did John Nash, the subject of the movie *A Beautiful Mind*, recover from schizophrenia?

3. What is the author's attitude about the field of mental health?

I just went to see the movie *Minority Report* a few weeks ago. As I watched Tom Cruise zoom and slug his way out of the traps closing in upon him, I felt strangely unnerved and anxious, yet also exhilarated. "I'm innocent," he declares when "Pre-Cogs" accuse him of a future murder. "You have a choice," chants Agatha the "Pre-Cog" hostage as Tom Cruise lifts his gun-laden hand towards his possible victim. "You have a choice." These words reverberate in my mind, as I recall similar words I once heard directed toward me.

No Joy in Psychosis

Twenty-four years ago, I was hospitalized for two years at McLean hospital in Belmont, Mass., diagnosed with schizophrenia, often considered a chronic, incurable disease of the mind. One day I was sitting at the center of the ward right next to the nurses' station. Sean K, a mental health worker, sat across from me on a folding chair. He was a big guy with wiry, black hair, a red, acned face, a paunch that hung over his belt, and large feet in heavy leather sandals. We were talking about Donna, who was in the quiet room communing with her voices, and about Gerry, who had been transferred to East House, not because he'd been violent, but because his refusal to take his medication made staff afraid that he might be. As we spoke, Sean clutched a clipboard to his knee with one big hand and stroked his chin with the other. It was midday, a busy time on the hall, and every once in a while our vision of each other was obscured by patients and staff walking by. "Well," he said, "Do you know what makes you different than most of the other patients here?"

"What?" I asked curiously.

Recovery for All

I consider myself a very lucky person. I don't think that I have some special talent or ability that has enabled me to recover [from schizophrenia] when so many others seem stuck in eternal patienthood. . . .

One of the elements that makes recovery possible is the regaining of one's belief in oneself. Patients are constantly indoctrinated with the message, explicit or implicit, that we are defective human beings who shouldn't aim too high. In fact, there are diagnostic labels, including "grandiosity" and "lack of insight," to remind us that our dreams and hopes are often seen as barriers to recovery instead of one of its vital components.

Judi Chamberlin, National Empowerment Center Newsletter, *1999, www.power2u.org/recovery/confessions.html.*

"You don't like it. You don't enjoy it," he said.

"What do you mean?" I asked, not sure of what he was talking about.

"Psychosis," he said. "You don't like it and you don't enjoy it. The others do. That is what makes you different than most of the other patients here."

The Way of Choice

According to popular culture, schizophrenia is a brain disease that is often acquired through heredity. It is characterized by persistent delusions and hallucinations that are largely suppressed only by the use of powerful anti-psychotic medications. This past year I watched a program on schizophrenia produced by *Nightline* and the prime image I recall from this program is one of a psychiatrist walking down the streets of a city, eyes straight ahead, intoning the words "Take the medication" while a homeless man with mental illness clutched at his sleeve. So, is the schizophrenia I was diagnosed with chronic? Can it only be controlled by the use of powerful anti-psychotic drugs, or is there another way, the way of choice, as Sean implied to me years ago as we sat together in mid-hall?

Apparently, of those diagnosed with schizophrenia, approximately 25% recover spontaneously and without treatment. One very publicized case of this kind of recovery is that of John Nash, whose story is told in the movie *A Beautiful Mind*. He didn't take medication. His recovery was the result of choice. "I became disillusioned with my illusions," he said in one interview. One of the most touching scenes in the movie takes place when Nash bids them farewell. A similar scene takes place at the end of the thinly disguised autobiographical account of schizophenia found in *I Never Promised You a Rose Garden*, when the protagonist Deborah turns her back on her illusions. "I am going to embrace the real world," she says to her illusions, "fully and completely. Goodbye. Goodbye."

Somehow, while watching *Minority Report* we knew that by affirming the capacity to choose, the Pre-Cog Agatha was affirming the fundamental nobility of the human soul. She knew that, as human beings, we are not mechanical drones caught helplessly in the twin fists of heredity and biochemistry. So much that we do in life has to do with attitude, expectations, and, ultimately, choice. Sean's words that day at McLean echoed in my mind and eventually transformed the sequence of my choices so that today no one would consider me to be a person with schizophrenia. Could it be that different words, damning words, caught other patients on the hall with the same diagnosis that I had, in a trap they could not escape?

No Easy Answers

There are no easy answers to the problem of schizophrenia, and I am the last person to want to add more burdens to the shoulders of people who suffer with it. I have often used medication temporarily when I thought it was necessary. However, I would say that 25% of people with schizophrenia, or even more, can find their way to full recovery by exercising their capacity to choose.

I am aware that within the field of mental health, there are those who would like to suppress this information and shut down the survivor movements that insist upon letting us know about it. But just because a fact makes you uncomfortable, requires you to work harder, or to seek more complex solutions to problems, doesn't make it untrue. The right to choose defines us as human beings.

People with schizophenia should be allowed to exercise the right to choose, because contrary to what some people would have us believe, they are as human as anyone else.

| "*'Willing' yourself out of schizophrenia [is] just about impossible.*"

Schizophrenics Cannot Choose to Cure Themselves

Sharon Begley

In the following viewpoint Sharon Begley describes the impact of schizophrenia through real-life examples of people afflicted with the disease. Even though doctors and scientists continue to learn more about the causes and symptoms of schizophrenia, there is still no cure. The author argues that schizophrenics cannot "will" themselves out of psychotic symptoms because they do not have the ability to distinguish between hallucinations and reality. Treatment with drugs can provide brief or sometimes lasting periods of recovery, but often at the expense of other side effects. Sharon Begley is a senior editor for Newsweek.

As you read, consider the following questions:

1. According to the author, at what point in life does schizophrenia usually strike?

2. What are the symptoms of schizophrenia as listed by Begley?

3. According to the author, how does the age of a person's father impact the likelihood he or she will develop schizophrenia?

The first time Chris Coles heard the voice, it spoke to him after midnight. In a gentle tone, it instructed him to meet his friend at a beach cove, right then, and apologize: Chris, the voice told him, had been planning to date the friend's girlfriend. Although Coles was planning no such thing, he did as instructed, arriving at the cove at 2 A.M. It was deserted. He dismissed the incident; imagination, after all, can play tricks in the twilight between waking and dreaming. But the voices kept intruding. Coles saw visions, too. At the beach near his California home, he often saw a profusion of whales and dolphins swimming onto the beach, and a golden Buddha glowing from the bushes by the dunes. "I also had delusions of grandeur," says Coles, now 47. "I felt that I had power over things in nature, influence over the whales and dolphins and waves. I thought I could make things happen magically in the water."

Donna Willey's visions came out of a darker world. She saw "bloody images, cut-up people, dismembered people," she says. Voices, too, began haunting her and, despite medication, still won't stop. "They say terrible things," says Willey, 43. "That what I'm doing is not important. They cuss and yell, trying to get me down, saying I shouldn't have done something that way. They're in my head, and they keep yelling." Even as she talks to a reporter in her office at the National Alliance for the Mentally Ill (NAMI) of Greater Chicago, the demons screech "You shouldn't say that," or "Don't say it that way." "The noise, the chaos in my head—it's hard to keep everything separate," she says.

The disease that came to be termed schizophrenia was first described by German psychiatrist Emil Kraepelin in the 1890s, but it remains one of the most tragic and mysterious of mental illnesses. Whether it brings the voices of heaven or of hell, it causes what must surely be the worst affliction a sentient, conscious being can suffer: the inability to tell what is real from what is imaginary. To the person with schizophrenia the voices and visions sound and look as authentic as the announcer on the radio and the furniture in the room. Some 2.5 million Americans have the disease, which transcends economic status, education, geography and even the loving kindness of family. Neither doctors nor scientists can accurately predict who will become schizophrenic. The cause is largely unknown. Although the disease almost surely arises from neurons that take a wrong turn during fetal development, it strikes people just on the cusp of adulthood. Whatever the cause, it seems not to change in frequency: the incidence of schizophrenia has remained at about 1 percent of the population for all the decades doctors have surveyed it. There is surely a genetic predisposition, but not an omnipotent one: when one identical twin has schizophrenia, his or her twin has the disease in fewer than half the cases. Treatment is improving, but a cure is not even on the horizon. . . .

Schizophrenia is marked by the persistent presence of at least two of these symptoms: delusions, hallucinations, frequently derailed or incoherent speech, hugely disorganized or catatonic behavior, or the absence of feeling or volition. If the delusions are especially bizarre, or the hallucinations consist of either a running commentary on what the person is doing or thinking, or multiple voices carrying on a conversation, then that alone qualifies the person as schizophrenic. In one subtype, catatonic schizophrenia, the patient often seems to be in a stupor, resisting all entreaties and instructions, or engages in purposeless movements, bizarre postures, exaggerated mannerisms or grimacing. . . .

In paranoid schizophrenia, the patient becomes convinced of beliefs at odds with reality, hears voices that aren't there or sees images that exist nowhere but in his mind. Eric Williamson has had paranoid schizophrenia for 15 of his 31 years. As a teen he was terrified that someone would enter his room at night, and so would barricade the door and dangle hangers from the window to alert him to intruders. He would eat only canned food, so paranoid was he that someone was trying to poison him. Once, when his mother walked past the kitchen table as he ate, he cried out, "Why did you put that poison in my soup!?" He soon lost his grip on reality altogether, telling her, "Look how my eyelashes are growing. That's because [my brother] is messing with me." . . .

Neuroscientists have now traced such hallucinations to malfunctions of the brain. In a 1995 study, researchers led by Drs. David Silbersweig and Emily Stern of Cornell Medical School teamed with colleagues in London to scan the brains of schizophrenics in the throes of hallucinations. As soon as an imagined voice spoke, or a vision appeared, a patient pressed a button. That told the scientists when to scrutinize the scans for abnormal activity. They found plenty. When one patient reported seeing dripping colors and severed heads, for instance, the parts of the sensory cortex that process movement, color and objects became active. . . .

When patients hear voices, the auditory cortex as well as the language-processing areas became active. "These regions process complex auditory, linguistic information, not just beeps or buzzes," says Silbersweig. The voices the patients heard were therefore as real to them as the conversations in the hallways they passed through en route to the lab.

Deep within the brain during hallucinations, structures involved in memory (the little sea-horse-shaped hippocampus), in emotions (the amygdala) and in consciousness (the thalamus) all flick on like streetlights at dusk. That suggests why hallucinations are packed with rare emotional power—the power to make Chris Coles ashamed enough to venture to a deserted beach at night, the power to make Eric Williamson so terrified he ate only canned food. Sensory signals are conveyed deep into the brain, where they link up with memories and emotions. The neuronal traffic might go the other way, too, with activity in the emotional and memory regions triggering voices and visions.

Why one person sees whales and another sees severed heads remains poorly understood. But the content of hallucinations probably reflects personal experience: in one patient the neuronal pathways activated during a hallucination run through the memories of seashore visits, while in another they intersect memories of pain and terror. . . . Soon after a relative tried to rape her at the age of 11, Joanne Verbanic became convinced that strangers were trying to break into her house. Fourteen years later ominous voices started telling her that her brother would be killed. "I thought I was being followed and my phone was being tapped," she says. "There was a hole in the ceiling of my closet, and I thought there was a wire up there. I thought they had installed microphones in my eyeglasses and a dental filling." Other voices told her to kill herself; at 25 she tried to throw herself from a moving car, but her husband yanked her back.

"What's so cruel about voices is that they come from your very own brain," says Carol North, now a respected psychiatrist and researcher at Washington University, who first heard voices when she was 16. "They know all your innermost secrets and the things that bother you most." North's voices tormented her about failing a neurophysiology exam. "That was a horrible thing for me. The voices said, 'Carol North got an F.' They'd say things like, 'She can't do it [get into medical school],' 'She's just not smart enough.'"

Another key brain area involved in schizophrenia is nearly silent. The Cornell/London brain-imaging study showed that schizophrenia is marked by abnormally low activity in the frontal lobes (just behind the forehead). These regions rein in the emotional system, provide insight and evaluate sensory information. They provide, in other words, a reality check. "You may need a double hit to suffer the psychotic symptoms of schizophrenia," says Silbersweig. "You need the aberrant sensory and emotional functioning, but you also need aberrant frontal-lobe function, which leaves you with no inhibition of these hallucinations and no reality check. That makes the hallucinations so believable."

The absence of a reality check makes "willing" yourself out of schizophrenia just about impossible. "It is very unlikely for somebody to will themselves to get better," says NIMH's [National Institute of Mental Health's Dr. Richard] Wyatt. . . . Even among people who have had their illness for decades, and who have periods of clarity (thanks to medication), only some learn to discriminate between the voices everyone hears and the voices only they can hear. Verbanic, who founded Schizophrenics Anonymous in 1985, had been hospitalized often enough to recognize her symptoms. While working on bankruptcies for Ford Motor Credit, "I thought the attorneys weren't really attorneys and the files were phony," she says. She asked a supervisor to take her to the hospital.

Identifying what happens in the brain during schizophrenic hallucinations is one step short of understanding why they happen. The old theory that cold, rejecting mothers make their children schizophrenic has long been discredited. Although the actual cause remains elusive, scientists know a few things. The age of the father matters. A 25-year-old has a 1-in-198 chance of fathering a child who will develop schizophrenia by 21, finds Dr. Dolores Malaspina of Columbia University. That risk nearly doubles when the father is 40, and triples when he passes 50. Viruses or stresses that interfere with a fetus's brain development also raise the risk; mothers who suffer rubella or malnutrition while pregnant have a greater chance of bearing children who develop the disease. And if there is schizophrenia in your family, you run a higher-than-average risk of developing it. [In 2001], researchers led by NIMH's Dr. Daniel Weinberger linked a gene on chromosome 22 to a near-doubled risk of schizophrenia. When the gene, called COMT, is abnormal, it effectively depletes the frontal lobes of the neurochemical dopamine. That can both unleash hallucinations and impair the brain's reality check. . . .

There is, as yet, no cure for schizophrenia, for drugs cannot unscramble tangled neuronal circuits. But drugs can quiet them. Those that give rise to the delusions and hallucinations of schizophrenia are awash in the neurochemical dopamine. Thorazine, an early antipsychotic, blocked dopamine receptors, with the result that dopamine had no effect on neurons. But since dopamine is also involved in movement, Thorazine leaves patients slow and stiff, "doing the Thorazine shuffle," says Suzanne Andriukaitis of NAMI. Dopamine also courses through circuits responsible for attention and pleasure, so Thorazine puts patients in a mental fog and deadens feelings. "The old drugs are a nuclear weapon against dopamine," says Dr. Peter Weiden of Downstate Medical Center in Brooklyn, N.Y. "They eliminate your sense of pleasure and reward. Patients lose their joy."

The new antipsychotics, called "atypicals," are more like smart bombs. Drugs including Clozaril, Risperdal, Zyprexa, Geodon and Seroquel target mainly the dopamine-flooded regions, so patients no longer feel as if the voices of 40 radio stations, as different as NPR [National Public Radio] and the local hip-hop station, are blaring in their ears. "The volume is softer, the speed is slower, it's making more sense," says Donna Willey. Although the voices and visions don't always disappear, the new drugs can allow people with schizophrenia to hold jobs and have families. Still, they increase appetite, and may alter metabolism, resulting in what NIMH's Wyatt calls "the enormous problem" of huge weight gain. Willey gains 20 pounds a year on Zyprexa, and has ballooned from 120 pounds to her current 280. That makes some reluctant to take the drugs. Another side effect is foggy thinking, the feeling that brain signals are trying to push through caramel. Patients may also lose their libido. For all the power of the new drugs, they are treatment and not cure.

Sometimes Chris Coles misses the angelic voices. "They said complimentary things," he remembers. "They were sweet voices, telling me about the sunrise or sunset." But Zyprexa and Seroquel have stilled the angels. Willey wishes her voices would fall silent. Although Zyprexa has hushed them, they still burst through perhaps once a day, especially during times of stress. And she still, 20 years after she first heard the voices, isn't always completely, totally sure that they're not real.

> "[Cognitive behavioral] therapy has genuinely given me the tools to fight and overcome any black mood should it try to engulf me again."

Cognitive Behavioral Therapy Is Effective

Justine Chase Gray

In the following viewpoint Justine Chase Gray recounts her positive experience with cognitive behavioral therapy (CBT). Gray, who sought professional help after being overcome with anxiety and depression, found the therapy to be simple, practical, and flexible. Gray was allowed the time she needed to share her feelings, and she was given tools to identify and challenge the negative and irrational thoughts that had been plaguing her. The author soon regained control of her life and her emotions, and she contends that CBT has changed her life for the better.

As you read, consider the following questions:

1. At what point did Gray realize that she needed professional help?

2. How did each of Gray's therapy sessions begin?

3. What kind of "homework" was the author assigned as part of her therapy?

I had come to a point where I no longer found joy in any-thing. Anything at all. I slept maybe two hours a night, doz-ing off finally at about 3 A.M. and jolting out of dreamless sleep at 5 or 6 A.M. with a start of sudden anxiety.

My concentration was extremely poor: at work I some-times "came to" staring blankly at my PC screen, unable to re-member what I had been doing for the past five minutes. The telephone would ring and I would start guiltily, expecting an-ger on the other end of the line. A couple of panic attacks a day were common, locked in the staff toilet, eyes clenched and trying to breathe myself back to calmness. I had stopped see-ing friends, feeling they were all secretly laughing at me. Even leaving the house was difficult. Surely everyone was staring at me. For the past two weeks my heart had been hammering constantly. My hands shook and sweated. My interests had dwindled to reading fiction, the only escape that still worked. Everything else seemed meaningless, even my relationship with my wonderful husband, who tried his best to help but was, ultimately, powerless to pull me back from the deep pit I'd found myself in.

One day I came home from work and collapsed onto the sofa, ready to escape into my book. I looked at it. I couldn't bring myself to pick it up. I didn't care about it. It didn't matter.

Seeking Professional Help

Now there was nothing left to care about I somehow realised that if I didn't get professional help I might soon be beyond it. I had always had an interest in all things to do with the mind, as my father had long-standing mental health problems, having been sectioned [institutionalized] for three separate suicide attempts. I realised I had an unhealthy outlook on life:

severe self-confidence problems, self-hatred, etc. I had even had a severe depressive episode after being declared in remission after a year of cancer treatment at the age of 20. Yet I had never sought professional help. I had always somehow stumbled through things. I came to be renowned among friends and work colleagues as someone who could take on any amount of work and stress and pull it off calmly and confidently. Needless to say, I was always a great actress and never felt half as confident as people gave me credit for being.

A bullying client at work, who had singled me out for special attention, now caused my slide into depression and anxiety. I couldn't handle it, and soon found myself unable to function.

Making the decision to seek help was, strangely, not a difficult one. I had heard about CBT [cognitive behavioral therapy] and wanted something that would give me the tools to deal with my own problems. I didn't want to be seeing a therapist for years talking about the past constantly, but wanted to move on, break whatever was holding me back from being happy. CBT seemed to be the thing to go for and I contacted Dr Alec Grant.

Establishing a Relationship

Within minutes of meeting Alec I thought I might just be able to trust him, and that was an extremely rare thing for me at that time. The way the small room was arranged was designed to make me feel comfortable, with no desk forming a barrier between us, as I had originally feared there might be. This made for sessions which made me feel equal with Alec, rather than engendering the doctor/patient relationship I had feared: the powerful and the powerless. I desperately needed someone who I not only felt had authority, knew how to deal with my problems, but could also be seen as a friend and confidant.

Feeling equal and valued by my therapist was hugely important for me at a time when I felt worthless and insignificant. Allowing me to begin to feel as though I could be as in control as my therapist, was wonderful. A simple thing, yet one which could have huge consequences.

Structure and Agenda-Setting

I was told clearly what would happen during the hour. Alec explained the basics of his practice of CBT, how it works, what it hoped to achieve, and about the homework that may be helpful for me to do. This simple explanation (with diagrams: essential tools for helping my mind, exhausted through terror and misery, to grasp even simple theories) again reinforced the feeling of equality, that here was an adult talking to another adult, rather than a doctor talking "down" to a patient, or a parent to a child. My hopes were raised. I reasoned that if my therapist could see that I was worth talking to, then perhaps others could too.

Every therapy session began with collaborative agenda-setting; a task which again helped give me a feeling of control and made me feel capable. It showed me that I could construct a meaningful dialogue and that the issues I wanted to discuss were worthwhile. This little challenge of one of my deeply held and damaging beliefs was vital, and every part of Alec's collaborative approach seemed geared towards breaking down my old and destructive thought patterns.

Sessions were as flexible as I needed them to be, in terms of content. What I had spoken about was always reflected back to me as Alec summed up my thoughts: "So what you're saying is . . .?" This gave me a feeling of confidence that this man was really listening to me and taking in what I was saying, which, at that point in my life, I thought no-one did.

Taking the History

At the initial session I was desperate to express to someone how much pain I was in, and launched into what I thought was going to be my rehearsed speech. Of course, faced with the situation I had wanted for so many years, I went to pieces and everything poured out in a jumble. After five minutes or so of listening patiently to my ramblings Alec asked, during one of my breathless pauses, whether I felt comfortable sitting the way I was. To tell the truth I had purposefully been sitting with my legs and arms uncrossed, as I had heard this was a signal that I was being open and honest and willing to talk, however uncomfortable it might be to sit like that. I also thought it might make me feel more comfortable, but I couldn't have been more wrong.

Alec, of course, had seen that this was causing me some amount of strain and let me know that I could sit however was most comfortable and to take my time. This simple statement put me much more at my ease. I could see he was intuitive and my confidence in him grew. I was able to seat myself comfortably (which, yes, did involve some crossing of body parts), collect myself and start with exactly what was bothering me at that time.

Alec gave history—taking much more time than I'd anticipated, for which I was hugely grateful as I had a lot to get off my chest. Before the sessions began I had read about CBT as being a fairly mechanistic process, and that the therapist would give between 20 and 30 minutes to taking a history and then get on with the therapy. Initially I had thought: "Great. Just what I need. Don't want to be lying on an old sofa discussing my father and my dreams for the next 15 years and getting nothing done." But when the day arrived I realised I needed time to talk about what had happened to me. And Alec gave me as much as I needed. Had I been rushed, I would have felt undermined. This would have simply served to strengthen my old beliefs that I was useless, boring, not worth listening to. The relationship, so desperately important between therapist and 'therapee', would have been irreparably ruined. I would have acquiesced to his demands to hurry my story along in

Cognitive Behavioural Therapy

All cognitive behavioural therapy (CBT) interventions rest on the idea that any of us can develop mental health difficulties if the meanings we attach to specific events are upsetting enough. The CBT approach helps people think about the way they think about themselves, the world and other people, and how these ideas then affect their thoughts, emotions or feelings, and behaviours.

CBT helps people change how they think (cognition) and what they do in response to their thinking (behaviour). It tries to help people explore whether there might be alternative ways of appraising situations.

It is not necessarily about thinking more rationally or more positively.

These changes can help people be more in control of their difficulties and reduce the emotional impact that unhelpful thinking patterns produce.

Nigel Short and Mark Hardcastle, Independent Nurse,
March 10, 2006.

my desperation to please, but he would have lost me. And I may have lost myself into the bargain.

I left the first session feeling happy, though it took me a few moments to identify the feeling as I hadn't experienced it in such a long time. I knew this was going to be hard work, and often frightening, but that things were going to change.

Identifying the Problem

Asked by Alec at the end of my first session to fill in depression and anxiety inventories at home, I agreed eagerly. I wanted to know exactly what was going on. Simply filling in the sheets had a calming effect: I could actually see things written down that I suffered from. This meant that someone before me had had the same experience. And seeing them written down made them somehow feel real, as if a higher authority had allowed me to be feeling this way. Even this simple exercise in diagnosis gave me hope; a thing I have since learnt is possibly the most important thing to hang on to.

Homework was negotiated every week, was hard work but often revelatory. Mostly it worked on challenging my beliefs about myself. A simple piece of homework such as "going to see someone you used to enjoy seeing" would have me quaking. But doing it made me feel as if I had achieved a feat of Olympian proportions. I could feel proud of myself—a thing which I had never before allowed myself. This constant challenging of my old feelings and thoughts gradually built up a picture of myself in my mind of a person who really was not that bad after all.

Being asked to do some reading was extremely helpful. The book Alec suggested, *Mind over Mood*, was clearly written and user-friendly, a term I see used much too often, but which really does describe it. Again, the book was filled with practical exercises, one of which, the thought record, I still use today when needed. Reading the book, the stories of people with stories like my own gave me an enormous sense of relief that I was not alone in feeling this way.

The Thought Record

This simple tool was again a wonderful way of examining, identifying and challenging feelings and old thoughts and beliefs by looking at what I was feeling, examining the thoughts that set these feelings in motion and then looking at what evidence existed to support these beliefs. No detailed instructions were needed, no fancy tools, no hard work, no extra energy or intelligence, just a piece of paper and pen. Writing down, making concrete, my thoughts and feelings, was a way of acknowledging them and making them real. In making them real, I could fight them. This, I believe, is the essence of the thought record, its triumph.

The first time I filled one in, even just the identifying and writing of my feelings felt like a relief. Having to think about the automatic thoughts which set off these feelings, and then having to describe them on paper was often a revelation. It's amazing how much of an effect seeing one's own honest thought, something as simple as, "He'll think I'm stupid", can have, an effect which includes beginning to see that this thought may not reflect the truth.

Having to look for evidence to back up my claims to being stupid was always harder than I thought it might be, and finding alternative explanations for others' behaviour seemed to be easier. I suddenly found a wonderfully simple tool to examine my feelings calmly, find out where they come from and see that there were many more likely reasons for whatever had happened calmed me hugely.

I still use the thought record, mostly in my head, as it has become almost second nature to run through my feelings, thoughts, evidence and so on if I am feeling particularly bad.

Creative Writing

Possibly the most important tool used for my homework sessions was creative writing. This was something I had always loved but had stopped doing through "fear of it being rubbish". One of the first writing assignments I agreed to do was rewrite a particularly traumatising event from my childhood. Write it how it had happened, then rewrite the end to make it happy, from my point of view. An event instantly came to mind; I knew it would be hard, a real challenge, and terribly frightening. And so it proved to be. So frightening in fact, that I found myself doing considerably more housework than was normal for me that week. Two days passed, then three, and before I knew it my next session was only a day away and I had been procrastinating all week. Excuses fluttered through my mind, vague thoughts of cancelling the session, but I knew I couldn't if I really wanted to do something about this.

Fifteen minutes later I was standing at the kitchen counter crying with laughter and relief. An amazing thing had happened. I had written the event quickly by hand in a notebook. The act of writing it down had brought me some relief, and I was surprised to see it in black and white. I could do this. Then I began work on rewriting the story. Writing my humiliation as a child out of it and replacing it with a "me" who was in control, strong, happy, good. As I wrote I could feel a smile creeping up on me. I carried on and soon I was grinning.

Finishing the story I burst out laughing. I laughed out loud, a thing I hadn't done for months. Neither had I cried properly for the last few months, though for the past six or seven I had been permanently on the verge of tears. Now the simple exercise of rewriting one moment in my life 25 years ago had me weeping tears of mirth in the kitchen.

A Revelation of Hope

I had no idea where this had come from, either the ending or the laughter, but suddenly I felt alright. As if a weight had been lifted. As if a light had gone on in my mind and everything was illuminated, rather than being cast in shadows as it had been for so long. It was astonishing. It was wonderful, it was, frankly, hilarious. Such a simple thing, such an amazing effect.

This is not to say, of course, that this meant the end of my therapy. But it gave me a revelation of hope. I could suddenly see that I was going to get through my pain and that I already had one of the tools I needed to help me accomplish this. And all after five days.

Writing continued to play an important role in my therapy and still does today, and that evening in my kitchen was a moment I shall never forget.

A Life-Changing Experience

I think to say that CBT changed my life is not an overstatement. It may sound melodramatic, a cheap line from a corny sitcom, but the therapy has genuinely given me the tools to fight and overcome any black mood should it try to engulf me again. The collaborative approach left me feeling empowered and in control of my emotions, my thoughts and my life, and the genuine warmth and concern expressed by Alec reawakened my belief that I was not such a bad person after all.

> "Negative thoughts recur throughout life.
> Instead of challenging them, . . . we
> should concentrate on identifying and
> committing to our values."

Accepting Negative Thoughts May Be More Effective than Cognitive Behavioral Therapy

John Cloud

In the following viewpoint Time *magazine staff writer John Cloud reports on a promising alternative to cognitive behavioral therapy (CBT): acceptance and commitment therapy, or ACT. Developed by psychologist Steven Hayes, ACT encourages patients to observe their thoughts without judgment. Rather than trying to change negative thinking patterns, which is the aim of CBT, ACT invites people to accept their thoughts and to feel their negative emotions. The therapy has proven successful in treating depression, anxiety, and addiction, Cloud explains.*

As you read, consider the following questions:

1. According to Cloud, what mental disorder did Steven Hayes suffer from when he was a young professor?

2. What is mindfulness, according to the author?

3. What turns pain into suffering, in Hayes's opinion?

Before he was an accomplished psychologist, Steven Hayes was a mental patient. His first panic attack came on suddenly, in 1978, as he sat in a psychology-department meeting at the University of North Carolina at Greensboro, where he was an assistant professor. The meeting had turned into one of those icy personal and philosophical debates common on campuses, but when Hayes tried to make a point, he couldn't speak. As everyone turned to him, his mouth could only open and close wordlessly, as though it were a broken toy. His heart raced, and he thought he might be having a heart attack. He was 29.

Eventually the attack subsided, but a week later he endured a similar episode in another meeting. Over the next two years, the panic attacks grew more frequent. Overwhelming feelings of anxiety colonized more and more of his life's terrain. By 1980, Hayes could lecture only with great difficulty, and he virtually never rode in an elevator, walked into a movie theater or ate in a restaurant. Because he couldn't teach much, he would often show films in his classes, and his hands would shake so badly that he could barely get the 8-mm film into the projector. As a student, he had earned his way from modest programs at colleges in California and West Virginia to an internship at Brown Medical School with esteemed psychologist David Barlow. Hayes had hoped to be a full professor by his early 30s, but what had been a promising career stalled.

Today Hayes, who turned 57 in August [2005], hasn't had a panic attack in a decade, and he is at the top of his field. A past president of the distinguished Association for Behavioral and Cognitive Therapies, he has written or co-written some 300 peer-reviewed articles and 27 books. Few psychologists are so well published. His most recent book, which he wrote with the help of author Spencer Smith, carries the grating self-help title *Get Out of Your Mind & Into Your Life*. But the book, which has helped thrust Hayes into a bitter debate in psychology, takes two highly unusual turns for a self-help manual: it says at the outset that its advice cannot cure the reader's pain (the first sentence is "People suffer."), and it advises sufferers not to fight negative feelings but to accept them as part of life. Happiness, the book says, is not normal.

If Hayes is correct, the way most of us think about psychology is wrong. In the years since Hayes suffered his first panic attacks, an approach called cognitive therapy has become the gold-standard treatment (with or without supplementary drugs) for a wide range of mental illnesses, from depression to post-traumatic stress disorder. And although a good cognitive therapist would never advise a panic patient merely to try to will away his anxiety, the main long-term strategy of cognitive therapy is to attack and ultimately change negative thoughts and beliefs rather than accept them. "I always screw up at work," you might think. Or "Everyone's looking at my fat stomach" or "I can't go to that meeting without having a drink." Part mentor, part coach, part scold, the cognitive therapist questions such beliefs: Do you really screw up at work all the time, or like most people, do you excel sometimes and fail sometimes? Is everyone really looking at your stomach, or are you overgeneralizing about the way people see you? The idea is that the therapist will help the patient develop new, more realistic beliefs.

But Hayes and other top researchers, especially Marsha Linehan and Robert Kohlenberg at the University of Washington in Seattle and Zindel Segal at the University of Toronto, are focusing less on how to manipulate the content of our thoughts and more on how to change their context—to modify the way we see thoughts and feelings so they can't push us around and control our behavior. Segal calls that process disidentifying with thoughts—seeing them not as who we are but as mere reactions. You think people always look at your stomach? Maybe so. Maybe it's huge. Maybe they don't; many of us are just hard on ourselves. But Hayes and like-minded therapists don't try to prove or disprove such thoughts. Whereas cognitive therapists speak of "cognitive errors" and "distorted interpretations," Hayes and the others teach mindfulness, the meditation-inspired practice of observing thoughts without getting entangled in them, approaching them as though they were leaves floating down a stream ("... I want coffee/I should work out/I'm depressed/We need milk ..."). Hayes is the most divisive and ambitious of the third-wave psychologists—so called because they are turning from the second wave of cognitive therapy, which itself largely subsumed the first wave of behavior therapy, devised in part by B.F. Skinner. (Behavior therapy, in turn, broke with the Freudian model by emphasizing observable behaviors over hidden meanings and feelings.)

Hayes and other third wavers say trying to correct negative thoughts can, paradoxically, intensify them, in the same way that a dieter who keeps telling himself "I really don't want the pizza" ends up obsessing about ... pizza. Rather, Hayes and the roughly 12,000 students and professionals who have been trained in his formal psychotherapy, which is called acceptance and commitment therapy (ACT), say we should acknowledge that negative thoughts recur throughout life. Instead of challenging them, Hayes says, we should concentrate on identifying and committing to our values. Once we become willing to feel negative emotions, he argues, we will find it easier to figure out what life should be about and get on with it. That's easier said than done, of course, but his point is that it's hard to think about the big things when we're trying so hard to regulate our thinking.

The cognitive model permeates the culture so thoroughly that many of us don't think to name it; it's just what psychologists do. When Phillip McGraw ("Dr. Phil") gives advice, for instance, much of it flows from a cognitive perspective. "Are you actively creating a toxic environment for yourself?" he asks on his website. "Or are the messages that you send yourself characterized by a rational and productive optimism?" Cognitive approaches were first developed in the 1950s and early '60s by two researchers working independently, University of Pennsylvania psychiatrist Aaron Beck, now 84, and Albert Ellis, 92, a New York City psychologist. The therapy's ascendance was rapid, particularly in the academy. Although many therapists still practice an evolved form of Freudian analysis called psychodynamic therapy, it's difficult to find a therapist trained in the past 15 years who didn't at least learn the cognitive model.

The debates between cognitive therapists and third-wave critics are sometimes arcane and petty, but few questions seem as elemental to psychology as whether we can accept interior torment or analyze our way out of it. Hayes was received at [the 2005] Association for Behavioral and Cognitive Therapies convention in Washington with reverence—and revulsion. It wasn't uncommon to see therapists gazing at him between presentations as though he were Yoda. (Hayes is given to numinous proclamations: "I see this acceptance conception, this mindfulness conception, as having the power to change the world.") But skeptics dog him everywhere. "He certainly has a following and even an entourage," says Providence College psychology professor Michael Spiegler. "But I do think some of what he does is cultlike in terms of having that kind of following, of having to agree wholeheartedly with it, or if you don't, you don't get it."

Sunset.

When you just read that word, no event occurred other than that your eyes moved across the page. But your mind may have raced off in any number of directions. Perhaps you thought of a beautiful sunset. And then maybe you thought of the beautiful sunset on the day your mother died, which might have evoked sadness.

Hayes uses such exercises to make the point that our thoughts can have unexpected consequences. *Get Out of Your*

Mind & Into Your Life illustrates that unreliability by quoting a 1998 Psychological Science Study in which 84 subjects were asked to hold a pendulum steady. Some were told not only to hold it steady but also not to move the pendulum sideways. But the latter group tended to move the pendulum sideways more often than the group told merely to keep it steady. Why? "Because thinking about not having it move [sideways] activates the very muscles that move it that way," Hayes and Smith write. To be sure, cognitive therapy doesn't ask people to suppress negative thoughts, but it does ask us to challenge them, to fix them.

By contrast, ACT tries to defuse the power of thoughts. Instead of saying "I'm depressed," it proposes saying "I'm having the thought that I'm depressed." Hayes isn't saying people don't really feel pain (he has felt plenty of it), but he believes we turn pain into suffering when we try to push it away. ACT therapists use metaphors to explain acceptance: Is it easier to drag a heavy weight on a chain behind you or to pick it up and walk with it held close?

The commitment part of acceptance and commitment therapy—living according to your values—sounds weightless at first. Many people are so depressed or lonely or caught up in daily life that they aren't sure what their values are. ACT therapists help you identify them with techniques like having you write your epitaph. They also ask you to verbalize your definition of being a good parent or a good worker. The therapist helps you think about what kind of things you want to learn before you die, how you want to spend your weekends, how you want to explore your faith. The point isn't to fill your calendar with Italian lessons and fishing trips but to recognize that, for instance, you like to fish because it means you spend time with your family or in the mountains or alone— "whatever is in fishing for you," says Hayes. One task in *Get Out of Your Mind* asks you to give yourself a score of 1 to 10 each week for 16 weeks to show how closely your everyday ac-

Acceptance and Commitment Therapy (ACT)

ACT differs from traditional *Cognitive Behavioral Therapy* (CBT) in that rather than trying to teach people to better control thoughts, feelings, sensations, memories and other private events (as CBT does), ACT focuses on what we can control more directly: our arms, legs and mouth. ACT teaches us to "just notice", accept, and embrace our private events, especially previously unwanted ones. ACT helps people get in contact with a transcendant sense of self known as "self-as-context"—the you that is always there observing and experiencing and yet distinct from one's thoughts, feelings, sensations, and memories. ACT helps people to clarify their personal values and to take action on them, bringing more vitality and meaning to their life in the process.

Wikipedia, "Acceptance and Commitment Therapy," April 23, 2006, http://en.wikipedia.org/wiki/Acceptance_and_Commitment_Therapy

tions comport with your values. If you really enjoy skiing with friends but end up watching TV alone every weekend, you get a 1. (But if you really love holing up with reruns of The O.C., go for it; ACT is pretty nonjudgmental.)

Now seems like a good time to stipulate that all this can sound vacuous and gaggingly self-helpy. But the scientific research on ACT has shown remarkable results so far. In the January [2006] edition of the journal *Behaviour Research and Therapy*, Hayes and four co-authors summarize 13 trials that compared ACT's effectiveness to that of other treatments after as long as a year. In 12 of the 13, ACT outperformed the other approaches. In two of the studies, depressed patients were randomly assigned to either cognitive therapy or ACT. After two months, the ACT patients scored an average of 59% lower on a depression scale. Those were small studies, just 39 patients total, but ACT has shown wide applicability. In a 2002 study, Hayes and a student looked at 70 hospitalized psychotics receiving the standard medication and counseling. Half were randomly assigned to four 45-min. ACT sessions; the other half formed the control. Four months later, the ACT patients had to be rehospitalized 50% less often. They actually admitted to more hallucinations than those in standard care, but ACT had reduced the believability of their hallucinations, which were now viewed more dispassionately. Hayes likes to say ACT effectively turned "I'm the Queen of Sheba" into "I'm having the thought that I'm the Queen of Sheba." The psychotics still heard voices; they just didn't act on them as much. They learned to hold their thoughts more lightly, increasing their psychological flexibility.

ACT has also shown promise in treating addiction. In one study, drug addicts reported less drug use with ACT than with a 12-step program. And ACT worked better than a nicotine patch for 67 smokers trying to quit. ACT encourages addicts to accept the urge to do drugs and the pain that will come when they stop—and then to work on figuring out what life means beyond getting high. ACT has also been used to help chronic-pain patients get back to their jobs faster. But perhaps the most noteworthy finding was that 27 institutionalized South African epileptics who had just nine hours of ACT in 2004 experienced significantly fewer and shorter seizures than those in a placebo treatment in which the therapist offered a supportive ear. Even Hayes, who is not usually overburdened with modesty, was startled by that finding. He could only hypothesize about why ACT might reduce seizures: "You teach people to walk right up to the moment they seize and watch it." Somehow, he suggests, that helps reduce biochemical arousal in those critical moments before the trigger of a seizure.

Obviously, Hayes isn't sure exactly how ACT is working in all those cases, but he believes it has something to do with learning to see our struggles—even seizures—as integral and valid parts of our lives. Recently, a San Francisco patient in ACT therapy e-mailed a plea for help to Hayes. "Just HOW I do that (live a valued, meaningful life) in the midst of disabling and oppressive private experience (anxiety, depression, lack of energy, inertia) is not clear to me. Does one just say the hell with it I will CHOOSE to live, to get into the life I value despite feeling awful 24 hours a day??"

Hayes had opened the e-mail at 3 A.M., after his newborn's cries had awakened him. At 4:04, he sent a long response that said, in part, "You are asking, 'Can I live a valued life, even with my pain?' Let me ask you a different question. What if you can't have the second without the first? What if to care the way you do care, means you will hurt. But not the heavy, stinky, evaluated, categorized, and predicted hurt that has crushed you. Rather the open, clear, knife-through-butter pain that comes from a mortal being who eventually will lose all and yet who cares. . . ."

Living by your values sounds great, but if no thought is good or bad, and no belief requires changing, what happens when the values are immoral? Should pedophiles live in accordance with their desires? Should an abused wife accept her husband's assaults? Eager to debate, Hayes has ready answers. "If somebody's gonna tell me, 'My value is sexually educating 8-year-olds,' I will not do therapy around that issue," he says. But while Hayes believes some people truly have pathological values, he says he has never had such a patient. "I've worked with rapists and things of that kind, but inside that I see people getting pushed around by their urges even when it's deeply against their values." The ACT theory is that once the pedophile stops trying to ignore or change his urges, he can defuse their power and make psychological room to think about what he can really do with his life. As for an abused spouse, *Get Out of Your Mind* says, "'Acceptance of abuse' is not what is called for. What may be called for is acceptance that you are in pain . . . and acceptance of the fear that will come from taking the necessary steps to stop the abuse." Acceptance, it turns out, can mean a lot of change.

For a time, in the 1990s, we seemed to think that curing mental illness was a matter of manipulating a couple of brain chemicals. But after decades of side effects and the recent debate over whether antidepressants carry suicide risk for teens, we have seen only marginal gains in public mental health. A 2002 study in *Prevention & Treatment* found that approximately 80% of the response to the six biggest antidepressants of the '90s was duplicated in control groups who got a sugar pill. So we may be ready for something different.

Hayes will have to do a great deal of research to show that ACT, like cognitive therapy, not only solves problems in the short term but prevents relapse. Hayes and his team believe they will get there, but even if they do, it seems likely that for ACT to go mainstream, it will have to shed its icky zealotry and grandiose predictions. ("We could get Muslims and Jews together in a workshop," Hayes said in Washington. "Our survival really is at stake.") Even so, Hayes may be crazy enough to pull it all together.

Periodical Bibliography

The following articles have been selected to supplement the diverse views presented in this chapter.

Leila Abboud — "Should Family Doctors Treat Serious Mental Illness?" *Wall Street Journal*, March 24, 2004.

Roy F. Baumeister — "The Lowdown on High Self-Esteem," *Los Angeles Times*, January 25, 2005.

Benedict Carey — "Mentors of the Mind," *Los Angeles Times*, June 18, 2001.

Paul J. Fink — "Rethinking Electroconvulsive Therapy," *Clinical Psychiatry News*, October 2004.

Bob Guldin — "A Treatment for Depression, or a Pain in the Neck?" *Public Citizen News*, September/October 2005.

Arline Kaplan — "Teacher of the Year Addresses Psychiatric Education, Schizophrenia Treatment," *Psychiatric Times*, February 1, 2006.

Katherine Lerer — "Twirling in Space: My Experience with Shock Therapy," *Psychology Today*, May 2000.

John S. March — "CBT: An Important Part of Treatment," *Clinical Psychiatry News*, July 2005.

Tara Pepper — "Talking to the Demons: Schizophrenia Is No Longer Seen as a Genetically Predetermined Disease," *Newsweek International*, December 12, 2005.

Louise Sharah — "A Patient's Story," *Australian Doctor*, March 31, 2006.

Nigel Short and Mark Hardcastle — "Cognitive Behavioural Therapy Explained," Clinical Section, *Independent Nurse*, March 10, 2006..

For Further Discussion

Chapter 1

1. Paul D. Lawrence maintains that mental disorders are prevalent in the United States and that they spring from biological as well as environmental stresses. Paul McHugh contends that researchers, relying on flawed studies, have overestimated the prevalence of mental illness in America. What kind of evidence does each author use to support his argument? Whose use of evidence do you find more convincing, and why?

2. Both Matthew W. Nelson and B.K. Eakman argue that health-care institutions have harmed or underserved the mentally ill and the vulnerable. On what major points do they disagree, however? In your opinion, whose argument is more compelling? Explain.

Chapter 2

1. Kenneth Richard Fox uses personal narrative and anecdotes to support his contention that the mentally ill may need to be given psychiatric treatment against their will. Thomas Szasz uses logic, historical allusions, and examples to make his case against the use of involuntary treatment. Which kind of support engages you more as a reader? Why?

2. After reading the viewpoints by Patrice G.W. Norton and Paula J. Caplan, do you think that traumatized military veterans should be encouraged to seek psychotherapy? Why or why not?

3. Do you agree with Peter D. Kramer that depression tends to be overromanticized as an element of the artistic temperament? Or do you believe, as Martin Gayford does,

that some mental disorders have a connection to creativity? Cite evidence from the viewpoints in defending your answer.

Chapter 3

1. After reading the viewpoints by Phyllis Schlafly and the President's New Freedom Commission on Mental Health, do you think that federally funded mandatory mental health screenings would help or harm children? Explain your answer.

2. Based on the viewpoints in this chapter and any other relevant material, do you think that society does too much or too little to address the needs of youths diagnosed with mental disorders? What, if any, accommodations do you think should be added or eliminated? Elaborate.

Chapter 4

1. Val Flint maintains that electroconvulsive therapy (ECT) is a safe and reliable treatment for certain severe forms of mental illness. Benedict Carey reports that ECT may not be as safe or effective as its promoters have reported. Flint is a nurse who specialized in ECT and mental health, while Carey is a staff writer for a major newspaper. How does knowing the authors' professions influence your assessment of their arguments?

2. Elizabeth A. Richter contends that she chose to be cured of schizophrenia and that a certain percentage of schizophrenics have that choice available to them. How do you think Sharon Begley would respond to Richter's viewpoint? Cite the viewpoints as you explain your answer.

3. Justine Chase Gray recounts her positive experience with cognitive behavioral therapy (CBT). According to John Cloud, what are some of the potential drawbacks of CBT? Do you think that acceptance and commitment therapy (ACT) is a viable alternative to CBT? Why or why not?

Organizations to Contact

American Psychiatric Association
1000 Wilson Blvd., Suite 1825, Arlington, VA   22209-3909
(703) 907-7300
e-mail: apa@psych.org
Web site: www.psych.org

An organization of psychiatrists dedicated to studying the nature, treatment, and prevention of mental disorders, the American Psychiatric Association helps create mental health policies, distributes information about psychiatry, and promotes psychiatric research and education. It publishes the *American Journal of Psychiatry* as well as the quarterly journal *Focus.*

American Psychological Association (APA)
750 First St. NE, Washington, DC   20002-4242
(800) 374-2721
Web site: www.apa.org

The APA is the world's largest association of psychologists. It produces numerous publications, including *Psychological Review, American Psychologist,* and the *Journal of Family Psychology.*

Bazelon Center for Mental Health Law
1101 Fifteenth St. NW, Suite 1212
Washington, DC   20005-5002
(202) 467-5730 • fax: (202) 223-0409
e-mail: webmaster@bazelon.org
Web site: www.bazelon.org

The Bazelon Center provides technical and legal assistance in selected court cases involving mental health law. It also advocates for increased consumer (patient) participation in the design and operation of mental health services. The center publishes handbooks, manuals, issue papers, and reports on key legal and policy issues related to mental health, including the issue of involuntary commitment.

Canadian Mental Health Association (CMHA)
8 King St. East, Suite 810
Toronto, ON   M5C 1B5   Canada
(416) 484-7750 • fax: (416) 484-4617
Web site: www.cmha.ca

The Canadian Mental Health Association assists people suffering from mental illness in finding the help they need to cope with crises, regain confidence, and return to their communities, families, and jobs. Its Web site includes a link to an archive of dozens of articles on mental illness, including "Mental Illness in the Family," "Youth and Psychosis," and "Bipolar Disorder."

Citizens Commission on Human Rights (CCHR)
6616 Sunset Blvd., Los Angeles, CA   90028
(800) 869-2247 • fax: (323) 467-4242
e-mail: humanrights@cchr.org
Web site: www.cchr.org

CCHR works to expose and eradicate criminal acts and human rights abuses in psychiatry. The organization believes that psychiatric drugs can cause insanity and violence. CCHR publishes numerous reports and booklets, including *The Drugging of "Post-Partum Depression"* and *Psychiatry, the Pharmaceutical Industry, and the FDA: A Destructive Alliance Endangering the Lives of Children.*

Depression and Bipolar Support Alliance
730 N. Franklin St., Suite 501, Chicago, IL   60601-7224
(800) 826-3632 • fax: (312) 642-7243
Web site: www.dbsalliance.org

The alliance provides support and advocacy for patients with depression and bipolar disorder. It believes these disorders are biochemical in nature and that no stigma should be placed on the people who suffer from them. It publishes dozens of reports and brochures, including "Myths and Facts and Depression and Bipolar Disorder" and "Psychotherapy: How It Works and How It Can Help."

National Alliance for the Mentally Ill (NAMI)
Colonial Palace Three, 2107 Wilson Blvd.
Arlington, VA   22201-3042
(800) 950-6264
Web site: www.nami.org

NAMI is a consumer advocacy and support organization that believes that severe mental illnesses are biological brain diseases and that mentally ill people should not be blamed or stigmatized for their condition. Its publications include the bimonthly newsletter *NAMI Advocate* and the brochure set *After a Suicide Attempt.*

National Empowerment Center (NEC)
599 Canal St., Lawrence, MA   01840
(800) 769-3728 • fax: (978) 681-6426
e-mail: info4@power2u.org
Web site: www.Power2u.org

The NEC is an organization run by current and former mental health patients. Its goal is to promote the philosophy that people who have been diagnosed with mental illnesses can recover and take charge of their own lives. The center publishes the *NEC Newsletter* and posts many newsletter articles on its Web site, including "People Can Recover from Mental Illness" and "Confessions of a Non-Compliant Patient."

National Institute of Mental Health (NIMH)
6001 Executive Blvd., Rm. 8184, MSC 9663
Bethesda, MD   20892-9663
(301) 443-4513 • fax: (301) 443-4279
e-mail: nimhinfo@nih.gov
Web site: www.nimh.nih.gov

The NIMH is a government agency that seeks to improve the treatment and prevention of mental illness through research in neuroscience, behavioral science, and genetics. It publishes fact sheets and booklets on several mental illnesses. The Surgeon General's landmark report on mental health is available on its Web site.

National Mental Health Association (NMHA)
2000 Beauregard St., 6th Fl., Alexandria, VA   22311
(703) 684-7722 • fax: (703) 684-5968
Web site: www.nmha.org

The association strives to promote mental health and prevent mental disorders through advocacy, education, research, and service. The NMHA publishes fact sheets, position statements, and pamphlets on mental health policy. Its Web site includes links to the report "Insufficient Combat Stress Help for U.S. Troops Faulted" and the pamphlet *Schizophrenia: What You Should Know.*

National Mental Health Consumers' Self-Help Clearinghouse
1211 Chestnut St., Suite 1207, Philadelphia, PA   19107
(215) 751-1810 • fax: (215) 636-6312
e-mail: info@mhselfhelp.org
Web site: www.mhselfhelp.org

The Clearinghouse provides information and technical assistance to the consumers' movement, a group of past and present consumers of mental health services (sometimes referred to as "survivors" or "ex-patients") who strive to improve the mental health system and help one another recover from mental illness. Its publications include background papers and political alerts on policy issues as well as the newsletter *Key Update.*

Treatment Advocacy Center (TAC)
200 N. Glebe Rd., Arlington, VA   22203
(703) 294-6001 • fax: (703) 294-6010

e-mail: info@psychlaws.org
Web site: www.psychlaws.org

The center is a national nonprofit organization working to eliminate barriers to timely treatment of severe mental illness. The center's founder, E. Fuller Torrey, is a renowned advocate of increased treatment for the mentally ill. His articles, including the briefing papers "The Effects of Involuntary Medication on Individuals with Schizophrenia and Manic-Depressive Illness" and "Violence and Severe Mental Illness" are available on the center's Web site. TAC also produces numerous other briefing papers and fact sheets.

Bibliography of Books

Diane R. Brown and Verna M. Keith, eds.
In and Out of Our Right Minds: The Mental Health of African American Women. New York: Columbia University Press, 2003.

Phyllis Chesler
Women and Madness. New York: Palgrave Macmillan, 2005.

Shirley Cohen
Targeting Autism: What We Know, Don't Know, and Can Do to Help Young Children with Autism Spectrum Disorder. Berkeley and Los Angeles: University of California Press, 2006.

Katherine Read Dunbar, ed.
At Issue: Antidepressants. San Diego: Greenhaven, 2005.

Penny Gray
The Madness of Our Lives: Experiences of Mental Breakdown and Recovery. London: Jessica Kingsley, 2006.

Joe Griffin and Ivan Tyrell
Human Givens: A New Approach to Emotional Health and Clear Thinking. Chalvington, UK: HG Publishers, 2003.

Gracelyn Guyol
Healing Depression and Bipolar Disorder Without Drugs. New York: Walker, 2006.

James Whitney Hicks
Fifty Signs of Mental Illness: A Guide to Understanding Mental Health. New Haven, CT: Yale University Press, 2006.

Janice Hunter
Jenkins, ed.

Schizophrenia, Culture, and Subjectivity: The Edge of Experience. New York: Cambridge University Press, 2004.

Richard Kadison
and Theresa Foy
DeGeronimo

College of the Overwhelmed: The Campus Mental Health Crisis and What to Do About It. San Francisco: Jossey-Bass, 2004.

Paul R. Kimmel
with Chris E.
Stout, eds.

Collateral Damage: How the U.S. War on Terrorism Is Harming American Mental Health. Westport, CT: Praeger, 2006.

Peter D. Kramer

Against Depression. New York: Viking, 2005.

Juan Jose
Lopes-Ibor et al.,
eds.

Disasters and Mental Health. Hoboken, NJ: Wiley, 2005.

Michael Martin

Teen Depression. San Diego: Lucent, 2004.

Theodor Millon

Masters of the Mind: Exploring the Story of Mental Illness, from Ancient Times to the New Millennium. Hoboken, NJ: Wiley, 2004.

Francis Mark
Mondimore

Depression, the Mood Disease. Baltimore: Johns Hopkins University Press, 2006.

Kim T. Mueser
and Susan
Gingerich

The Complete Family Guide to Schizophrenia: Helping Your Loved One Get the Most Out of Life. New York: Guilford, 2006.

Demitri Papalos
and Jennifer
Papalos
*The Bipolar Child: The Definitive and
Reassuring Guide to Childhood's Most
Misunderstood Disorder.* New York:
Broadway, 2006.

Mark Pollard
In Small Doses: A Memoir About Accepting and Living with Bipolar Disorder. Mill Valley, CA: Vision Books
International, 2004.

Tim Rowan
*Solution-Oriented Therapy for Chronic
and Severe Mental Illness.* New York:
Norton, 2003.

Sarah Russell
*A Lifelong Journey: Staying Well with
Manic Depression/Bipolar Disorder.*
Toronto: Warwick, 2006.

Norman Sartorius
and Hugh Schulze
Reducing the Stigma of Mental Illness.
New York: Cambridge University
Press, 2005.

Jennifer A.
Schaler, ed.
Szasz Under Fire: The Psychiatric Abolitionist Faces His Critics. Chicago:
Open Court, 2004.

Timothy Scott
*America Fooled: The Truth About Antidepressants, Antipsychotics, and How
We've Been Deceived.* Victoria, TX:
Argo, 2006.

Susan Senator
*Making Peace with Autism: One
Family's Story of Struggle, Discovery,
and Unexpected Gifts.* Boston: Trumpeter, 2006.

Meredith F. Small	*Culture of Our Discontent: Beyond the Medical Model of Mental Illness.* Washington, DC: National Academies Press, 2006.
Thomas Szasz	*The Manufacture of Madness: A Comparative Study of the Inquisition and the Mental Health Movement.* Syracuse, NY: Syracuse University Press, 1997.
Graham Thornicraft	*Shunned: Discrimination Against People with Mental Illness.* New York: Oxford University Press, 2006.
Sami Timimi	*Naughty Boys: Anti-Social Behavior, ADHA, and the Role of Culture.* New York: Palgrave Macmillan, 2005.
E. Fuller Torrey	*Surviving Schizophrenia: A Manual for Families, Patients, and Providers.* New York: HarperCollins, 2006.
Tina Zahn with Wanda Dyson	*Why I Jumped: My True Story of Postpartum Depression, Dramatic Rescue, and Return to Hope.* Grand Rapids, MI: Revell, 2006.

Index